ANDRÉ-PHILIPPE BOULANGER TROTTIER

# 50 Crazy Founders Stories

*Be inspired by remarkable journeys and challenge everything you think you knew about yourself.*

Copyright © 2024 by André-Philippe Boulanger Trottier

All rights reserved. No part of this publication may be reproduced, stored or transmitted in any form or by any means, electronic, mechanical, photocopying, recording, scanning, or otherwise without written permission from the publisher. It is illegal to copy this book, post it to a website, or distribute it by any other means without permission.

André-Philippe Boulanger Trottier asserts the moral right to be identified as the author of this work.

André-Philippe Boulanger Trottier has no responsibility for the persistence or accuracy of URLs for external or third-party Internet Websites referred to in this publication and does not guarantee that any content on such Websites is, or will remain, accurate or appropriate.

Designations used by companies to distinguish their products are often claimed as trademarks. All brand names and product names used in this book and on its cover are trade names, service marks, trademarks and registered trademarks of their respective owners. The publishers and the book are not associated with any product or vendor mentioned in this book. None of the companies referenced within the book have endorsed the book.

First edition

This book was professionally typeset on Reedsy.
Find out more at reedsy.com

It's time to learn how to use what you already have, and be as you really are.

- BRIANNA WIEST

# Contents

## I  50 Crazy Founders Stories

| | |
|---|---|
| Prologue | 3 |
| Cliff Weitzman | 5 |
|    From Dyslexia to Disruption | 5 |
| Paige Mycoskie | 9 |
|    From Surf Shop to Fashion Empire | 9 |
| Katrina Lake | 15 |
|    Sewing Seeds of Ambition | 15 |
| Ivan Zhao | 20 |
|    The Blank Page Pitch | 20 |
| Whitney Wolfe Herd | 25 |
|    Redefining Online Connections | 25 |
| Marc Lore | 30 |
|    The E-Commerce Maverick | 30 |
| Justin Kan | 35 |
|    From Lifecasting to Billion-Dollar Triumph | 35 |
| Kara Goldin | 40 |
|    Turning Health Challenges into a Thriving Business | 40 |
| Joshua Browder | 45 |
|    The Disruptor Behind the World's First Robot Lawyer | 45 |
| Anne Wojcicki | 49 |
|    Revolutionizing Health Through Genetics | 49 |

| | |
|---|---:|
| Ben Chestnut | 54 |
|    Turning Setbacks into Billions | 54 |
| Sophia Amoruso | 59 |
|    From Dumpster Diving to Building an Empire | 59 |
| Adriana Gascoigne | 64 |
|    Bridging the Gender Gap in Tech | 64 |
| Sam Altman | 69 |
|    The Visionary Behind OpenAI | 69 |
| Stewart Butterfield | 73 |
|    From Failed Game to Billion-Dollar Communication Platform | 73 |
| Eileen Fisher | 78 |
|    Crafting a Timeless Fashion Legacy | 78 |
| Tristan Walker | 83 |
|    Shaping the Future of Grooming and Healthcare | 83 |
| Tope Awotona | 88 |
|    Scheduling Success Through Adversity | 88 |
| Jennifer Hyman | 93 |
|    Revolutionizing Fashion with Rent the Runway | 93 |
| Payal Kadakia | 98 |
|    Dancing Her Way to Disruptive Innovation | 98 |
| Travis Kalanick | 102 |
|    Navigating the Ride of a Lifetime | 102 |
| Marc Barros | 107 |
|    Capturing Adventure with Contour | 107 |
| Lisa Price | 112 |
|    From Kitchen Alchemist to Beauty Mogul | 112 |
| David Heath | 117 |
|    Revolutionizing Comfort and Giving with Bombas | 117 |
| James Park | 121 |
|    From Harvard Dropout to Fitness Tech Titan | 121 |

| | |
|---|---|
| Alexa Von Tobel | 125 |
|   From Ivy League to Fintech Queen | 125 |
| Tom Preston-Werner | 130 |
|   From Code Dreamer to GitHub Guru | 130 |
| Alekseï Pajitnov | 134 |
|   From Soviet Labs to Global Obsession | 134 |
| Jessica Herrin | 139 |
|   Empowering Women Through Innovation | 139 |
| Chris Barton | 142 |
|   The Early Inventor | 142 |
| Yvon Chouinard | 146 |
|   Adventure Roots: From Maine to California | 146 |
| Julie Wainwright | 151 |
|   Reinventing Resilience and Luxury | 151 |
| Brian Chesky | 155 |
|   From Air Mattresses to IPO | 155 |
| Daniel Ek | 160 |
|   The Maestro Behind Spotify's Symphony | 160 |
|   Conclusion | 162 |
| Rachel Carlson | 163 |
|   From Boardroom to Blackboard | 163 |
| Brian Halligan | 168 |
|   The Mastermind Behind the Inbound Revolution | 168 |
| Joachim Sauter & Pavel Mayer | 172 |
|   The Billion Dollar Code | 172 |
| Sara Blakely | 175 |
|   Reinventing Shapewear | 175 |
| Neil Patel | 179 |
|   Digital Marketing Dynamo Redefining Success | 179 |
| Benjamin Francis | 184 |
|   From Garage Startup to Fitness Empire | 184 |

| | |
|---|---|
| Tony Xu | 189 |
|   From Takeout to Triumph | 189 |
|   Bootstrapping Beginnings | 189 |
|   Visionary Insights: | 191 |
| Arianna Huffington | 193 |
|   Redefining Media and Wellness with The Huffington Post and Thrive Global | 193 |
| Jimmy Donaldson | 198 |
|   Mastering the Art of Viral Content with MrBeast | 198 |
| Tobi Lütke | 203 |
|   Coding His Way to E-Commerce Revolution | 203 |
| Michelle Zatlyn | 208 |
|   From Canada to Silicon Valley: A Journey Begins | 208 |
| Ryan Trahan | 212 |
|   Crafting a YouTube Empire with Creativity and Grit | 212 |
| Julia Hartz & Kevin Hartz | 216 |
|   From Separate Paths to a Unified Vision | 216 |
| Emily Weiss | 220 |
|   Revolutionizing Beauty with Glossier | 220 |
| Marc Benioff | 225 |
|   Early Life and the Seeds of Innovation | 225 |
| Evan Spiegel | 230 |
|   Pioneering Ephemeral Communication | 230 |

# I

# 50 Crazy Founders Stories

# Prologue

If you find yourself wavering on the edge of a new venture, hesitant to take that leap, or if you're already fully immersed in your passion project but facing seemingly insurmountable challenges, then this book is your beacon.

In the vast sea of obstacles that stand between us and our dreams, it's easy to perceive others as giants, wondering why success seems reserved for them alone.

Yet, it's crucial to recognize that beneath their achievements, they are just as human as we are. Their journeys are marked by stumbles and setbacks, far from flawless.

So, whether you're grappling with self-doubt or confronting seemingly insurmountable hurdles, remember that you are not alone. Every setback is a lesson, every obstacle a chance to grow. Ultimately, the true victory lies not in the absence of challenges but in the choices we make in response to them.

Let this book be your source of inspiration and empowerment as you navigate the twists and turns of your own journey. Embrace every part, as it is in the struggle that we find our greatest strength.

Embrace the narratives of these 50 individuals, each marked by their own trials and tribulations. Let their stories serve as a testament to your own journey, a reminder that you, too, are navigating your own path.

And that, more than anything, the biggest win of all will always be the win of choice.

# Cliff Weitzman

## From Dyslexia to Disruption

Born in 1995, Weitzman's early years were marked by the challenges of learning English and coping with a learning disability. His struggles in school landed him in special needs programs, with teachers and peers doubting his potential. Yet, it was here, amidst the struggle and doubt, that the seeds of his future success were sown.

## Discovering Audiobooks

Determined to beat the odds, young Cliff found solace and strategy in an unexpected place: audiobooks. Inspired by listening to "Harry Potter" audiobooks, he not only mastered English but discovered a powerful tool to aid his learning. This was a turning point. While others saw limitations, Weitzman saw opportunities.

## A New World at Brown University

Despite the naysayers, Cliff's tenacity paid off. His relentless pursuit of knowledge and refusal to accept defeat earned him a place at Brown University. But the challenges only grew. The rigorous academic environment demanded more than traditional study methods could offer. Cliff, however, was not one to shy away from a challenge. He realized he needed a more efficient way to absorb the increasing volume of information.

## Birth of Speechify

Between classes and late into the nights, Weitzman began working on a solution that would change his life—and many others—forever. He developed the initial version of a text-to-speech app, which allowed him to listen to his lecture notes. What started as a personal tool quickly attracted the attention of his classmates. Fully capable students began asking for the app, recognizing its potential to enhance their own study routines.

In a twist he hadn't anticipated, what began as a personal necessity turned into a product with mass appeal. Encouraged by the demand, Weitzman refined the app and launched it to the public, naming it Speechify. The app's premise was simple yet revolutionary: converting written text into spoken words, making reading accessible to everyone, especially those with learning disabilities.

## Building an Empire

The response to Speechify was nothing short of phenomenal. What started as a tool for personal use evolved into a company employing over 100 people, offering support in 14 different languages. Speechify quickly rose to the top of the App Store's magazine and newspaper category, even surpassing stalwarts like The New York Times. Cliff Weitzman, once a special needs student with little hope of attending college, was now a Forbes 30 Under 30 honoree, recognized for his groundbreaking work in assistive technology.

## Overcoming Adversity

Cliff's journey wasn't without obstacles. Funding was a constant struggle in the early days, as investors were skeptical of the market potential for assistive technology. Yet, Weitzman's unyielding passion and personal connection to the product convinced them otherwise. His commitment to improving the lives of those with dyslexia and other learning disabilities drove him to innovate continuously, ensuring that Speechify remained at the cutting edge of technology.

## Impact and Legacy

Speechify's impact extends far beyond its original target audience. Students, professionals, and casual readers worldwide have embraced the app for its ability to enhance productivity and efficiency. Schools and universities have integrated Speechify into their accessibility programs, further broadening its reach.

Cliff Weitzman's story is a testament to the power of resilience, innovation, and empathy. By turning his personal challenges into a source of inspiration, he has empowered millions to overcome their own obstacles. His vision for the future of voice technology continues to drive Speechify forward, setting new standards for what assistive technology can achieve.

His journey from a struggling student to a tech visionary is a story of grit, ingenuity, and unexpected triumphs. His ability to turn personal adversity into a universal solution has not only revolutionized the way people read but has also redefined the potential of assistive technology. Cliff's story is an inspiring reminder that with determination and innovation, one can transform challenges into groundbreaking success.

# Paige Mycoskie

## From Surf Shop to Fashion Empire

Born in 1980 in Texas, Paige Mycoskie grew up with an entrepreneurial spirit that manifested early in life. She learned the value of hard work and reward through experiences like selling goods as a child. This foundation set the stage for her future success.

## The Unexpected Journey Begins

Paige Mycoskie's journey to becoming one of the wealthiest self-made women started in the most unexpected of places: the reality TV show, "The Amazing Race." Competing with her older brother Blake, Paige and her team finished third, an achievement that earned her a trip to Los Angeles. What was supposed to be a brief vacation turned into a life-altering decision. Captivated by the city's vibrant energy and creative spirit, Paige decided to quit college and move to Los Angeles full-time, abandoning her original plans and diving headfirst into an uncertain future.

## Finding Inspiration in Venice Beach

With no clear plan, Paige took a job at a surf shop in Venice Beach, immersing herself in the laid-back, sun-soaked lifestyle. Her days were spent surfing, but it was the world of retail that truly captured her imagination. Despite having no prior design experience, Paige began experimenting with creating her own clothes after hours. She sourced second-hand T-shirts and transformed them with her handmade designs, drawing inspiration from the vintage styles and colors of the 1970s. Her first surfing experience on the West Coast sparked her love for the California lifestyle, which would become a cornerstone of her brand.

## A Spark of Genius

The turning point came when Paige decided to test the waters by purchasing a $500 stand to sell her T-shirts at a local street fair. To her amazement, she sold out her entire inventory in one day, making $8,000. This overwhelming success was a clear sign: she had found her calling. The very next day, Paige quit her job at the surf shop and founded Aviator Nation, a California lifestyle brand that would soon become iconic for its retro-inspired clothing.

## Building Aviator Nation

Aviator Nation's journey from a small stand in Venice Beach to a major fashion brand is a testament to Paige's relentless drive and creative vision. Her unique take on vintage fashion—characterized by bright colors, bold stripes, and a distinctly 1970s vibe—resonated with a growing audience. The brand's commitment to quality and authenticity set it apart in a market flooded with mass-produced clothing. Paige's hands-on approach, personally overseeing every design, ensured that each piece carried her signature touch.

## The Pandemic Boom

While many businesses struggled during the pandemic, Aviator Nation thrived. Faced with the sudden shutdown due to California's shelter-in-place order, Paige launched a 24-hour flash sale on the website, announcing that every dollar would go directly to the employees to keep them paid through the shutdown. The response was overwhelming; Aviator Nation had its biggest sales day ever, bringing in $1.5 million. Paige reflected on this moment, saying, "I was immediately relieved, because I had money now in the bank to pay the people, even though they weren't going to be working." This money allowed Paige to pay over 200 employees during the months of shutdown, demonstrating her resilience and ability to adapt in crisis.

## Lessons from The Amazing Race

The resilience and adaptability Paige demonstrated on "The Amazing Race" were key to her success. The competitive spirit and determination to overcome obstacles were traits she carried into her business endeavors. Her brother Blake, who competed with her on the show, went on to found Toms Shoes, a $600 million brand known for its one-for-one model of giving. The entrepreneurial spirit clearly runs in the family, with both siblings achieving remarkable success in their respective ventures.

## Staying True to Her Vision

Throughout Aviator Nation's growth, Paige remained committed to her original vision. She focused on creating a brand that wasn't just about clothing, but about a lifestyle—a feeling of freedom and adventure that resonated deeply with her customers. Her designs became synonymous with the California dream, a blend of sun, surf, and laid-back coolness.

In an interview, Paige reflected on her journey, emphasizing the importance of staying authentic. "I wanted to create something that wasn't just about fashion but about a feeling—a sense of freedom and adventure," she explained. "Every piece I design is meant to inspire people to live their best lives, to be active, and to embrace the moment."

## Overcoming Challenges

The path to success was not without its hurdles. In the early days, Paige faced financial constraints and the pressure of scaling her business while maintaining the handcrafted quality that defined her brand. She recalls long nights spent sewing and the struggle to balance creativity with the demands of running a business. Despite these challenges, her passion and dedication never wavered. Being open-minded and enjoying the process were key elements to her approach.

## Cultural Impact and Celebrity Endorsement

Aviator Nation's rise to fame was marked by its growing presence in popular culture. Celebrities and influencers began wearing her designs, and the brand was featured in major fashion magazines. Mycoskie's creations became synonymous with the West Coast lifestyle, attracting a loyal following that extended beyond California.

One of the pivotal moments in Aviator Nation's journey came when Mycoskie decided to open her first retail store in Venice Beach, California. The store's success validated her vision and marked a significant milestone in the brand's growth. It became a hub for the local community, reflecting the vibrant, laid-back ethos of Aviator Nation.

## Insights from a Visionary

Reflecting on her journey, Paige shared insights that underscore her entrepreneurial philosophy. "You have to be willing to take risks and embrace the unknown," she said. "Success doesn't come from playing it safe; it comes from pushing boundaries and staying true to your passion."

Paige also emphasized the importance of community and customer connection. "Building a brand is about more than just selling products. It's about creating a community and fostering a sense of belonging. At Aviator Nation, our customers are part of a larger family, and their feedback and support have been instrumental in our success."

## Legacy and Future Vision

Paige Mycoskie's impact on the fashion industry is profound. Through Aviator Nation, she has created a brand that transcends clothing, embodying a lifestyle and a sense of community. Her commitment to quality, authenticity, and a positive ethos has set her apart as a visionary entrepreneur.

Looking ahead, Mycoskie envisions expanding Aviator Nation's reach while maintaining its core values. She aims to continue creating designs that inspire and connect with people on a deeper level. Her journey is a testament to the power of passion, creativity, and resilience in building a successful brand.

## Conclusion

Paige Mycoskie's story is a powerful example of how a blend of creativity, authenticity, and entrepreneurial spirit can create a cultural phenomenon. From her early days as an athlete and designer to the founder of a beloved lifestyle brand, Mycoskie's journey is a source of inspiration for aspiring entrepreneurs. Her ability to stay true to her vision and overcome challenges serves as a reminder that with dedication and a clear sense of purpose, it is possible to turn a dream into reality.

# Katrina Lake

## Sewing Seeds of Ambition

Born in 1982 in San Francisco, California, Katrina Lake grew up with a deep appreciation for education and hard work, instilled by her Japanese immigrant mother and her doctor father. Her journey to becoming a successful entrepreneur began with an ambition to bridge technology and retail in a way that had never been done before. Lake pursued her undergraduate degree at Stanford University, majoring in economics. However, it wasn't until she enrolled at Harvard Business School that her entrepreneurial vision began to take shape.

## The Epiphany of Personalized Retail

During her time at Harvard, Lake noticed a significant gap in the retail market. She realized that while shopping online was convenient, it often lacked the personalized touch and satisfaction of in-store shopping. This observation sparked the idea for Stitch Fix, an online personal styling service that would blend data science and human touch to provide personalized fashion recommendations. Despite having no background in fashion or technology, Lake was determined to bring her vision to life.

## From Apartment Dreams to Startup Reality

In 2011, while still a student, Lake started Stitch Fix from her apartment. She faced significant skepticism from potential investors, many of whom doubted that a young woman with no fashion or tech experience could revolutionize the retail industry. Lake's early pitches were often met with doubt, but she persisted, driven by a strong belief in her idea. She utilized her own savings and sought small investments from friends and family to get the business off the ground.

Lake's approach was unique: clients would fill out a detailed style profile, and Stitch Fix's algorithm, combined with human stylists, would curate a personalized box of clothing and accessories. Clients could try on the items at home, keep what they liked, and send back the rest. This innovative model combined the convenience of online shopping with the personalization of a boutique experience.

## Battling Biases and Breaking Barriers

Building Stitch Fix was far from easy. Lake faced numerous challenges, from logistical hurdles to scaling operations. In the early days, she personally packed and shipped boxes, often working late into the night. She also had to prove that Stitch Fix could be profitable, a challenge in the notoriously low-margin retail industry. Additionally, as a female entrepreneur in a male-dominated venture capital world, Lake had to overcome gender biases and prove her credibility repeatedly.

Despite these obstacles, Stitch Fix's unique value proposition began to resonate with customers. The company's emphasis on personalization and convenience quickly gained traction, and word-of-mouth referrals helped drive growth. Lake's persistence paid off when she finally secured significant venture capital funding, allowing her to expand the team and operations.

## The IPO Leap: Making History

In 2017, Stitch Fix went public, making Katrina Lake the youngest female founder to take a company public at the age of 34. The IPO was a resounding success, and Stitch Fix's stock surged, highlighting the company's strong market position and growth potential. Lake's achievement was not only a personal triumph but also a significant milestone for female entrepreneurs everywhere.

Reflecting on this achievement, Lake shared, "It was kind of an impulsive thing. What was amazing was how many other people felt it was meaningful to them as well. At the time I didn't love when people described me as a female CEO—I just want to be a great CEO; I don't need the 'female' tag on there. But I realized in that moment, in that IPO picture, how important it is. I think about myself growing up: When I was a little girl, there were no examples of somebody who looks like me doing that. Now I cherish and really show who I am in a way that's authentic so that other people out there who don't feel they see themselves in business leaders can feel there's a path for them."

## Blazing a Trail with Data and Design

Lake's journey offers valuable insights into the importance of perseverance, innovation, and customer-centric thinking. "Success is about solving problems in a way that truly serves your customers," Lake said in an interview. Her approach to integrating data science with personal styling set a new standard in the retail industry and demonstrated the power of combining technology with a human touch.

Lake also emphasizes the importance of resilience and adaptability.

"The journey of building a business is filled with ups and downs. It's crucial to stay focused on your vision and be willing to adapt and learn from every challenge," she advises aspiring entrepreneurs.

## Redefining Entrepreneurial Archetypes

In an interview with Forbes, Lake highlighted that entrepreneurial potential isn't determined by traditional qualifications. Success can come from unconventional entrepreneurial visions, and entrepreneurship offers diverse pathways, not just high-risk ventures. "Entrepreneurial journeys can be unique and non-linear. Personal backgrounds or education don't limit entrepreneurial capabilities. Embracing entrepreneurship means embracing varied risk profiles," she shared. This perspective has inspired many to see entrepreneurship as inclusive and welcoming of different perspectives and approaches.

## Innovating Beyond Fashion

Katrina Lake's impact on the retail industry is profound. She has not only transformed how people shop for clothes but also paved the way for future innovations in personalized retail experiences. Her success with Stitch Fix has inspired countless entrepreneurs to pursue their own visions, demonstrating that with determination and a customer-focused approach, it's possible to disrupt even the most established industries.

## Conclusion

Looking ahead, Lake's commitment to continuous improvement and her drive to leverage technology in new ways ensure that Stitch Fix will remain at the forefront of retail innovation. Her legacy is not just in the success of her company, but in the inspiration she provides to future entrepreneurs—showing that with creativity, resilience, and a clear vision, they too can carve out their own path and make a lasting impact on their industries.

# Ivan Zhao

## The Blank Page Pitch

Born in the mid-1980s in China, Ivan Zhao's story began with his family's emigration to Canada when he was young, offering him a new world of opportunities. Growing up in Vancouver, Zhao exhibited a keen interest in design and technology, passions that would become the cornerstone of his career.

Zhao pursued a degree in Cognitive Science at the University of British Columbia. Here, he delved into the intricacies of human-computer interaction, combining his love for design with a deep understanding of how people think and work. This blend of skills and interests would later culminate in the creation of Notion, an all-in-one workspace app that would revolutionize productivity tools.

## The Birth of Notion

After graduating, Zhao worked as a designer at Inkling, an ed-tech startup in San Francisco. It was during this time that he realized the fragmented nature of productivity tools. He envisioned a unified workspace where all aspects of a project—notes, tasks, databases, and collaboration—could coexist seamlessly. In 2013, he co-founded

Notion Labs with Simon Last, driven by this vision of an integrated, user-friendly workspace.

Notion's journey began with a small, dedicated team working out of Zhao's apartment. The initial version of Notion was a web-based tool that combined elements of a note-taking app, a task manager, and a database. However, the road to success was fraught with challenges.

## Overcoming Obstacles

The early years of Notion were marked by numerous setbacks. In 2015, the company was almost out of money. Zhao had founded Notion on the idea that a word processor should be as versatile as a blank piece of paper. His pitch was unconventional, involving a lengthy digression into the origins of paper. This unique approach impressed Josh Kopelman, cofounder of First Round Capital, who provided the largest check in their $2 million seed round in 2013.

Kopelman recalled, "I remember walking out and thinking, 'This is different from any founder pitch I've ever taken.' There was no screenshot, no mockup. It was very conceptual, but I felt like I understood at the highest level what he wanted to do."

However, Kopelman was in the minority. Two years later, many still didn't understand Notion, and Zhao struggled to explain it compellingly. Few saw the need for a tool to design personalized computer programs. Zhao even felt that some of the early users from First Round Capital were using Notion "out of pity," highlighting the uphill battle he faced in gaining broader acceptance.

Refusing to give up, Zhao and Last spent the next two years rebuilding Notion from scratch. They moved to Kyoto, Japan, to live cheaply while they reimagined the product. During this period, Zhao and Last focused on creating a tool that was not only powerful but also delightfully simple to use. They drew inspiration from early computing pioneers like Alan Kay and Douglas Engelbart, aiming to build a tool that would empower people to think and work better.

## The Turning Point

In 2018, Notion 2.0 was launched, and it quickly gained traction. Its unique blend of flexibility and functionality resonated with users, and it wasn't long before Notion became a sensation among startups, freelancers, and large enterprises alike. The app's ability to serve as a notes app, task manager, and collaboration tool, all in one, set it apart from the competition.

One of the most compelling aspects of Notion's success was its organic growth. Without relying heavily on traditional marketing, Notion grew through word of mouth, as users praised its versatility and design. This grassroots approach not only saved costs but also created a passionate and loyal user base.

## Building a Community

Zhao's commitment to user experience and community engagement became a defining feature of Notion's growth strategy. He listened intently to user feedback, continually iterating on the product to meet their needs. This user-centric approach fostered a strong community of advocates who shared their workflows, templates, and success stories, further driving Notion's popularity.

One notable anecdote involves the story of a small business owner who, after struggling to manage multiple tools, found Notion to be the perfect solution. The seamless integration of various functions allowed the business to streamline operations, saving time and money. Stories like these highlighted the transformative impact of Zhao's creation.

## Expanding Horizons

With its success firmly established, Notion began to expand its capabilities. Zhao and his team introduced features such as offline mode, API integrations, and advanced collaboration tools. These enhancements solidified Notion's position as a comprehensive productivity platform, capable of serving diverse needs across different industries.

In a 2020 interview with Forbes, Zhao reflected on Notion's rapid growth and the company's vision. "Our goal has always been to create a tool that feels like it was built for the individual, even as it scales to accommodate the needs of large teams," Zhao explained. He emphasized the importance of user experience, stating, "We want Notion to be the Lego kit for your ideas, where you can build anything you imagine without friction."

In 2020, Notion achieved unicorn status, valued at over $2 billion. The app became a staple in the productivity toolkits of millions worldwide, from individual users to large corporations. Zhao's vision of a unified workspace was now a reality, transforming how people organized their work and lives.

## Legacy and Future Vision

Ivan Zhao's journey from a curious young designer to the founder of a revolutionary productivity tool is a story of perseverance, innovation, and an unwavering commitment to user experience. Notion's impact on the way people work and collaborate is profound, offering a glimpse into the future of productivity tools.

Looking ahead, Zhao envisions Notion becoming even more integrated into the fabric of daily work life. He aims to continue pushing the boundaries of what a productivity tool can be, exploring new ways to make information management and collaboration more intuitive and efficient.

## Conclusion

Ivan Zhao's story is a testament to the power of vision and resilience. Through his journey, he has demonstrated that with dedication and a user-centric approach, it is possible to create a product that not only meets but exceeds the needs of its users. Notion's success is a reflection of Zhao's passion for design and his belief in the potential of technology to improve how we work and think. His story is an inspiring reminder that even the most ambitious dreams can become reality with the right blend of innovation, perseverance, and empathy.

# Whitney Wolfe Herd

## Redefining Online Connections

Born in Salt Lake City, Utah, in 1989, Whitney Wolfe Herd grew up with a love for creativity and entrepreneurship. She attended Southern Methodist University, where she studied international studies. Her early career included working in marketing and sales, which honed her skills in understanding consumer behavior and market dynamics.

## The Tinder Chapter: Triumphs and Tribulations

In 2012, Wolfe Herd joined the team at Hatch Labs, where she co-founded the dating app Tinder. She played a pivotal role in marketing and branding Tinder, contributing to its rapid growth and success. However, her time at Tinder was marked by significant challenges. Wolfe Herd faced internal conflicts and eventually filed a lawsuit against Tinder for sexual harassment and discrimination, a case that was settled out of court. The experience left her determined to create a safer and more empowering environment for women in the tech industry.

## The Birth of Bumble: Revolutionizing Online Dating

Fueled by her desire to make online dating a more respectful and empowering experience, Wolfe Herd founded Bumble in 2014. The idea was revolutionary: an online dating platform where women make the first move. This concept aimed to challenge the gender norms prevalent in the dating world and provide women with more control over their online interactions. Despite facing skepticism from potential investors and competitors, Wolfe Herd was undeterred. She secured initial funding with the help of Russian billionaire Andrey Andreev, who provided the resources and support needed to launch Bumble.

## Building Bumble: A Community of Empowerment

Building Bumble was no easy feat. Wolfe Herd faced the dual challenges of establishing a new brand in a competitive market and overcoming the stigma associated with her departure from Tinder. She worked tirelessly to differentiate Bumble by emphasizing its core values of respect, equality, and empowerment. The platform's unique features, such as women making the first move and robust anti-harassment policies, resonated with users and quickly set Bumble apart from its competitors.

Wolfe Herd's marketing prowess was instrumental in Bumble's early success. She leveraged social media, influencer partnerships, and college campus events to drive user engagement and brand loyalty. Her efforts paid off, and Bumble's user base grew rapidly, attracting millions of users worldwide.

## Overcoming Challenges: Legal Battles and Expansion

As Bumble grew, Wolfe Herd faced numerous challenges, including navigating the complexities of scaling a tech startup and managing a growing team. She also dealt with legal battles, including a lawsuit from Match Group, Tinder's parent company, which accused Bumble of patent infringement and misuse of intellectual property. Despite these obstacles, Wolfe Herd remained focused on her vision and continued to innovate and expand Bumble's offerings.

In addition to dating, Bumble launched Bumble BFF and Bumble Bizz, extending its platform to help users find friends and professional connections. These expansions reinforced Bumble's mission to empower women in all aspects of their lives, from personal relationships to career networking.

## IPO and Recognition: Making History

In February 2021, Bumble went public, making Whitney Wolfe Herd the youngest female founder to take a company public at the age of 31. The IPO was a historic success, with Bumble's valuation soaring and Wolfe Herd becoming a billionaire. This milestone was not only a personal triumph but also a significant moment for female entrepreneurs globally, showcasing the potential for women-led companies to achieve remarkable success.

Reflecting on this achievement, Wolfe Herd shared, "I don't need to justify myself anymore. I'm f-cking done," she said, highlighting her determination to move past her experiences at Tinder and focus on building a positive future. "Why am I cleaning up somebody else's drama? Women are always cleaning up somebody else's mess."

## Insights and Vision: Empowerment Through Innovation

Wolfe Herd's journey offers valuable insights into the importance of resilience, innovation, and a strong value-driven approach. "Building a company isn't just about profits; it's about creating something that makes a positive impact," she stated in an interview. Her commitment to empowering women and fostering respectful online interactions set Bumble apart and created a loyal user base.

"When you believe in something strongly, it's crucial to stick with it, even when faced with doubt and adversity," she advises aspiring entrepreneurs. Her ability to navigate challenges and remain focused on her mission has been key to her success.

## The Impact and Future of Bumble: Beyond Dating

Whitney Wolfe Herd's impact on the tech industry and online dating is profound. By prioritizing women's empowerment and safety, she has redefined the online dating experience and set new standards for the industry. Bumble's success has inspired other platforms to adopt similar features, leading to broader changes in how online interactions are managed.

Looking ahead, Wolfe Herd continues to drive Bumble's growth and innovation. She remains committed to expanding Bumble's reach and exploring new ways to support women's empowerment in various aspects of life. Her vision for Bumble extends beyond dating, aiming to create a global community where women feel empowered and respected.

## A Commitment to Social Responsibility

In an open letter on Bumble's website, Wolfe Herd expressed her dedication to solving societal problems and advancing gender equality. "When I founded Bumble, it was because I saw a problem I wanted to help solve," she wrote. "For all the advances women had been making in workplaces and corridors of power, the gender dynamics of dating and romance still seemed so outdated. I thought, what if I could flip that on its head? What if women made the first move, and sent the first message?"

Wolfe Herd's commitment to social responsibility extends to broader societal issues. "In 2020, as the U.S. faces a long-overdue reckoning with centuries of anti-black racism, we're committed to ensuring our activism is truly intersectional. Black Lives Matter at Bumble, on our platform and across our business, today and always," she stated.

## Conclusion

Wolfe Herd's ability to navigate legal battles, societal skepticism, and the competitive tech landscape with unwavering commitment to her values highlights her exceptional leadership. By prioritizing transparency, fairness, and user safety, she built Bumble into a platform that millions trust and love. Her historic achievement of taking Bumble public and becoming the youngest female founder to do so underscores her role as a trailblazer for female entrepreneurs everywhere.

# Marc Lore

## The E-Commerce Maverick

Born in 1971 in Staten Island, New York, Marc Lore grew up with the values of hard work and determination instilled by his supportive family. His journey into the world of e-commerce was marked by determination and resilience. After quitting his stable Wall Street job, Lore ventured into launching several e-commerce brands. Despite his best efforts, these initial ventures saw minimal success. However, these early setbacks only fueled Lore's ambition and sharpened his entrepreneurial skills.

## Diapers.com: A Revolution in Baby Products

In 2005, Lore co-founded Diapers.com (originally 1800Diapers) with his childhood friend Vinit Bharara. The concept was straightforward yet revolutionary: an online store dedicated to baby products with a focus on exceptional customer service. Diapers.com thrived by offering fast delivery and competitive prices, capturing the attention of parents across the United States. Lore's innovative logistics and keen understanding of customer needs turned Diapers.com into a rapidly growing success.

## The Price War with Amazon

Diapers.com's meteoric rise did not go unnoticed. Jeff Bezos, the founder of Amazon, saw Lore's venture as a potential threat. Bezos approached Lore with an acquisition offer, but Lore, confident in his vision and strategy, refused to sell. This decision triggered a fierce price war between Diapers.com and Amazon. Amazon slashed prices and ramped up their own baby product offerings, putting immense pressure on Diapers.com.

## A Hard-Fought Sale to Amazon

Despite Lore's fierce resilience, the price war drained Diapers.com's resources. Realizing the toll it was taking on his company, Lore eventually accepted Amazon's acquisition offer in 2010, selling Diapers.com's parent company, Quidsi, for $545 million. This sale was bittersweet for Lore. While it was a significant financial achievement, it also left him with a lingering grudge against Bezos and a desire to prove himself once more.

## Jet.com: A New Challenger Emerges

Lore wasn't done. Armed with the cash from his exit and a burning drive to challenge Amazon, he launched Jet.com in 2014. Jet.com was designed with a revolutionary business model, focusing on dynamic pricing and operational efficiency to offer lower prices. It quickly became known as the Costco of the internet, attracting millions of users and raising substantial investment. Lore's vision for Jet.com was clear: to create a formidable competitor to Amazon.

## Walmart's Strategic Acquisition

Jet.com's rapid growth and innovative approach caught the attention of retail giant Walmart. In 2016, just two years after its launch, Walmart acquired Jet.com for $3.3 billion. This acquisition was one of the largest in e-commerce history and marked a significant milestone in Lore's career. With the vast resources of Walmart behind him, Lore was poised to take on Amazon more directly.

## Overhauling Walmart's Online Presence

Taking on the role of President and CEO of Walmart U.S. eCommerce, Lore set out to transform Walmart's online presence. He implemented strategic initiatives to enhance the user experience, expand product offerings, and integrate Jet.com's advanced technology into Walmart's operations. Under Lore's leadership, Walmart's e-commerce sales grew exponentially, positioning the company as a formidable competitor to Amazon.

## Insights on Transparency, Trust, and Fairness

Lore's journey is a testament to his resilience and strategic thinking. In interviews, he emphasized the importance of transparency, trust, and fairness in business. He advocated for corporate transparency, sharing comprehensive information with employees to empower them and foster a connected company culture. Lore also highlighted the importance of trusting employees and compensating them fairly, ensuring that everyone at the same level received equal pay and stock options.

## The Toll of Entrepreneurship

Lore's success with Jet.com came at a personal cost. The intense workload and pressure led to burnout and physical symptoms, such as nausea. His experience reflects the harsh reality of entrepreneurship, where extreme dedication and hard work can take a toll on one's health and well-being.

## The Visionary Future: Telosa

Marc Lore's impact on the retail industry is profound. His innovative approaches to e-commerce and customer service have set new standards and inspired countless entrepreneurs. As he continues to explore new ventures, Lore's vision for the future remains as bold and ambitious as ever. One of his most notable initiatives is his plan to build a "city of the future" called Telosa, aimed at creating a sustainable and inclusive community using cutting-edge technology.

## Conclusion

Marc Lore's story is a powerful example of visionary leadership and relentless innovation. From his early struggles with e-commerce ventures to transforming Walmart's online presence and envisioning futuristic cities, Lore's journey is marked by bold decisions and a deep understanding of the future of retail and technology. His ability to inspire and drive change serves as a beacon for entrepreneurs and innovators worldwide.

# Justin Kan

## From Lifecasting to Billion-Dollar Triumph

Born in 1983 in Seattle, Washington, Justin Kan grew up with the values of hard work and perseverance instilled by his Chinese immigrant parents. His early fascination with technology and innovation set the stage for a career that would revolutionize live streaming.

## From Yale Graduate to Lifecaster

After graduating from Yale with a degree in Physics and Philosophy, Kan embarked on a venture as audacious as it was innovative. In 2007, he launched Justin.tv, a platform where he would "lifecast" every moment of his daily life using a camera affixed to his cap. The concept quickly captured the world's attention, with media outlets clamoring for interviews. The sight of a young entrepreneur broadcasting his every move was both fascinating and groundbreaking.

## The Pivot to Broader Horizons

Realizing the broader potential of the platform, Kan evolved Justin.tv in 2007, allowing others to also live stream their lives. This pivot proved to be a masterstroke. Within a year, Justin.tv boasted over 30,000 broadcasting accounts. Among the various categories of content, gaming emerged as the standout, amassing a huge and dedicated fan base.

## Birth of Twitch: Gaming's New Frontier

On June 6th, 2011, Kan made a decisive move. Recognizing the explosive growth and passionate community around gaming, he launched Twitch.tv, a live streaming service dedicated exclusively to gaming enthusiasts. The impact was immediate and profound. By 2013, Twitch was drawing over 35 million unique visitors every month, becoming a sensation in the gaming community.

## A Billion-Dollar Vision

As Twitch's dominance grew, so did the whispers of potential acquisitions. In a bold and strategic move, Kan shuttered the original Justin.tv platform, rebranding his entire company to Twitch Interactive. This decision underscored his belief in the transformative power of Twitch and its potential to redefine entertainment. The gamble paid off in monumental fashion. In 2014, Amazon announced that it had acquired Twitch for a jaw-dropping $970 million. This acquisition was a testament to Twitch's meteoric rise and its potential to reshape the future of media and entertainment.

## Venturing Beyond Twitch

Following the success of Twitch, Kan continued to push the boundaries of innovation. He co-founded Atrium, a technology-enabled law firm aimed at revolutionizing legal services for startups. Although Atrium eventually shut down in 2020, it provided valuable lessons and insights that Kan carried forward into his subsequent endeavors. Kan's journey also led him into the venture capital space. As a partner at Y Combinator, one of the world's most renowned startup accelerators, he has mentored and invested in numerous startups, helping shape the next generation of entrepreneurs. His experience and insights have made him a respected figure in the tech community.

## Struggles and Triumphs

Kan's journey was not without its challenges. In a candid reflection on Medium, he shared: "I struggled with alcohol addiction for over 20 years, among other destructive habits. Founders need to build better habits, not just better products. In 2013, my services startup Exec. was failing. I started drinking because I felt an incredible amount of internalized guilt. I felt like an imposter, and that the failure of my company would reveal to the world who I really was. I also felt guilt for the people I had hired, and the grand promises to investors that I would have to break."

## Lessons from Early Ventures

In a motivational speech to students, Kan recounted his initial startup venture, Kiko, which predated Twitch's success. Embracing the concept of starting with a "shitty first draft" in both writing and startup ventures, Kan's team found early-stage investment crucial through Y

Combinator's Summer Founders program. Despite struggling, they successfully sold Kiko on eBay for $258,100, a pivot point that led to new opportunities and eventually to the creation of Justin.tv and Twitch.

## Reflections from the Front Lines

In a 2019 interview with Forbes, Kan reflected on his entrepreneurial journey and the lessons he learned along the way. "You have to be willing to pivot and iterate constantly. The startup world is unpredictable, and the ability to adapt is crucial," he said. Kan also emphasized the significance of community and user feedback, stating, "Building a product that resonates with users requires listening to them and understanding their needs. At Twitch, our community was everything, and their input shaped the platform in meaningful ways."

## A Legacy of Innovation

Justin Kan's impact on the tech industry is undeniable. From pioneering live streaming with Justin.tv to revolutionizing gaming content with Twitch, his contributions have left an indelible mark. His journey illustrates the power of perseverance and the importance of embracing change. Looking ahead, Kan continues to explore new opportunities and support emerging entrepreneurs. His vision extends beyond just creating successful companies; he aims to foster a culture of innovation and resilience in the tech community.

## Conclusion

Justin Kan's story is a testament to the transformative power of entrepreneurship. His ability to navigate challenges, pivot strategically, and build thriving communities has set him apart as a visionary leader. Kan's journey serves as an inspiration for aspiring entrepreneurs, reminding them that with determination, adaptability, and a user-centric approach, they too can turn ambitious dreams into reality.

# Kara Goldin

## Turning Health Challenges into a Thriving Business

Born in Minneapolis in 1967, Goldin had a successful career in tech and media, including high-profile roles at AOL, where she helped grow its e-commerce and shopping business. Despite her corporate success, Goldin faced a significant personal challenge: her health. She struggled with weight gain, low energy, and skin issues, and no diet or exercise regimen seemed to help.

### Quenching Thirst with a Vision

Goldin's turning point came when she decided to eliminate diet soda from her routine and switch to drinking water. However, she found plain water boring and missed the flavors she loved. Inspired by her frustration, she began experimenting with adding slices of fruit to her water at home. This simple change had a dramatic impact: her health began to improve rapidly. She lost weight, her skin cleared up, and her energy levels soared. Realizing that she was onto something significant, Goldin wondered why there weren't any flavored waters on the market without sweeteners or additives.

## From Soda Woes to Water Wonders

In 2005, without any prior experience in the beverage industry, Goldin decided to take a leap of faith. She began working on her idea to create a truly healthy flavored water. Despite being a mother of four and having no formal training in the beverage industry, she was determined to bring her vision to life. Goldin and her husband, Theo, worked tirelessly in their kitchen, experimenting with different fruit infusions to perfect the formula for what would become Hint Water.

Her first big break came when she convinced a local Whole Foods buyer to stock her product. Goldin personally delivered the cases to the store, only to find out later that they had sold out within a few hours. This validation fueled her determination to push forward.

## Defying the Giants

Building Hint was fraught with challenges. The beverage industry is notoriously tough, dominated by giants like Coca-Cola and PepsiCo. Goldin faced skepticism from potential investors and retailers who doubted that a mom with no industry experience could disrupt the market. Moreover, she encountered significant production and distribution hurdles. Finding manufacturers willing to produce her product without preservatives or sweeteners was incredibly challenging.

One of the most dramatic moments in Hint's early days came when a large order from Whole Foods was delayed due to manufacturing issues. With no time to waste, Goldin and her husband rented a truck and drove across the country to deliver the products themselves, ensuring that Hint stayed on store shelves. This level of dedication and hands-on problem-solving exemplified Goldin's relentless commitment to her vision.

## Taking Flight and Gaining Fame

Despite these early struggles, Goldin's persistence paid off. Hint began to gain traction, winning over health-conscious consumers who were looking for a genuinely healthy alternative to sugary drinks. Goldin's innovative approach to marketing, including leveraging social media and influencer partnerships, helped build a loyal customer base.

Goldin's ability to adapt and innovate was crucial. When major retailers were slow to adopt Hint, she pivoted to a direct-to-consumer model, allowing her to reach customers directly and build a robust online presence. This move not only boosted sales but also provided valuable consumer insights that helped refine the product line.

## Surprising Success and Recognition

Hint's success grew exponentially. By 2015, Hint was a household name among health-conscious consumers, and Goldin's story became an inspiration to aspiring entrepreneurs. In 2017, Hint Water became available on every American Airlines flight, a major milestone that showcased the brand's widespread appeal. Goldin's vision of providing a healthy, flavorful alternative to sugary beverages had become a reality.

Goldin's achievements have been recognized with numerous awards, and she has been featured in major media outlets, sharing her journey from corporate executive to health advocate and successful entrepreneur. Her memoir, "Undaunted: Overcoming Doubts and Doubters," became a bestseller, further cementing her status as a role model for overcoming adversity.

## Innovate, Adapt, and Thrive

Kara Goldin's journey offers profound insights into the power of resilience, innovation, and staying true to one's mission. "Success is not about having all the answers; it's about being willing to figure things out as you go," Goldin said in an interview. Her ability to navigate challenges and pivot when necessary has been key to Hint's success.

Goldin also emphasizes the importance of passion and perseverance. "When you believe in your product and its potential to make a difference, that passion becomes contagious," she advises aspiring entrepreneurs. Her unwavering belief in the health benefits of Hint Water has been the driving force behind her journey.

## Beyond the Bottle

Kara Goldin's impact on the beverage industry and health advocacy is significant. She has not only disrupted the market but also inspired a movement towards healthier drinking habits. Hint's success has encouraged other entrepreneurs to pursue their visions and challenge industry norms.

Looking ahead, Goldin continues to drive Hint's growth and innovation. She remains committed to expanding Hint's product line and reach, exploring new flavors and health-focused beverages. Her vision extends beyond beverages, aiming to promote overall wellness and healthy living.

## Conclusion

Kara Goldin's journey is more than just the story of a successful entrepreneur; it's a narrative of resilience, innovation, and the relentless pursuit of a healthier lifestyle. From battling personal health challenges to creating a product that revolutionized the beverage industry, Goldin exemplifies how adversity can be a powerful catalyst for change. Her commitment to transparency, health, and consumer education has not only carved out a niche in a saturated market but also inspired a movement towards better living.

As Hint continues to grow and expand into new areas of health and wellness, Goldin's journey reminds us that the most significant innovations often come from personal experiences and challenges. Her story is a powerful reminder that with a clear vision, unwavering dedication, and a little bit of creativity, we can overcome any obstacle and make a meaningful difference in the world. Kara Goldin's legacy is not just in the success of Hint but in the countless lives she has touched and inspired along the way.

# Joshua Browder

## The Disruptor Behind the World's First Robot Lawyer

Born in 1997 in London, Joshua Browder's journey began with his encounters with the frustrating and often bewildering world of parking tickets as a teenager. The complex legal jargon and cumbersome appeal processes seemed designed to trip up the average citizen. It was during these encounters with bureaucratic red tape that Browder, still in high school, found his calling. He decided to harness technology to make legal assistance accessible to everyone, thus sowing the seeds for his future enterprise.

### A Teenage Entrepreneur

At just 18, Browder's frustration with the parking ticket system led him to develop a simple chatbot. This chatbot, which he dubbed DoNotPay, could help users contest parking fines by generating appeal letters automatically. What started as a modest project to help himself and friends quickly gained traction. In just a few months, DoNotPay had successfully contested over 160,000 parking tickets across London and New York, saving users millions in fines. The success was both astonishing and indicative of a vast, untapped need for accessible legal assistance.

## Stanford and Beyond

Browder's innovative spirit didn't stop there. He moved to the United States to study computer science and economics at Stanford University. Here, surrounded by the vibrant entrepreneurial ecosystem of Silicon Valley, he saw the broader potential of his creation. Browder envisioned DoNotPay not just as a tool for contesting parking tickets but as a platform for democratizing legal services.

While juggling his studies, Browder expanded DoNotPay's capabilities. The app began to tackle a variety of legal issues, from helping users get refunds for flights to fighting unfair bank charges. Each new feature was born out of a keen understanding of everyday legal frustrations and a desire to empower individuals against bureaucratic giants.

## The Robot Lawyer

Browder's big break came when he rebranded DoNotPay as "the world's first robot lawyer." This bold claim captured the public's imagination and highlighted the app's potential to revolutionize the legal industry. Using artificial intelligence, DoNotPay could provide instant legal advice and draft documents for a wide range of issues, all for a fraction of the cost of traditional legal services.

One of the app's most dramatic successes came when it helped thousands of people avoid evictions during the COVID-19 pandemic. By generating the necessary legal documents and offering real-time advice, DoNotPay enabled users to navigate the complex legal landscape without the need for expensive lawyers. This not only saved homes but also showcased the app's potential for profound social impact.

## Overcoming Challenges

Browder's journey was not without its challenges. The legal industry, known for its resistance to change, viewed DoNotPay with suspicion and, at times, outright hostility. Critics questioned the reliability of AI in legal contexts and raised concerns about the ethical implications of automated legal advice. Undeterred, Browder focused on improving the app's accuracy and expanding its functionalities, constantly iterating to ensure that DoNotPay could stand up to scrutiny.

Funding was another hurdle. Convincing investors to back a robot lawyer was no easy feat. However, Browder's tenacity and the app's growing user base eventually attracted significant venture capital. This financial backing allowed DoNotPay to scale rapidly and continually refine its technology.

## The Human Impact

Beyond the statistics and the technological marvels, Browder's work has had a deeply human impact. Stories of individuals who managed to avoid crippling debts, secure refunds, or even save their homes thanks to DoNotPay are plentiful. These anecdotes underscore the app's mission: to level the playing field and make justice accessible to all.

One particularly poignant story is that of a single mother who faced eviction during the pandemic. Using DoNotPay, she was able to generate the necessary legal documents to contest her eviction and stay in her home. Her gratitude and relief were a testament to the app's real-world impact and the difference it made in people's lives.

## Conclusion

Joshua Browder's relentless pursuit of accessible legal solutions has positioned him as a visionary in the legal tech space. His journey, marked by innovation, resilience, and a deep commitment to social justice, serves as an inspiration to aspiring entrepreneurs and disruptors. As DoNotPay continues to evolve, Browder's vision of a world where legal assistance is universally accessible draws closer to reality, promising a fairer and more just society for all.

# Anne Wojcicki

## Revolutionizing Health Through Genetics

Born in Palo Alto, California, in 1973, Anne Wojcicki grew up in an academic environment fostered by her parents—a Stanford physics professor and an educator. This setting nurtured her love for learning and inquiry. Wojcicki attended Yale University, where she earned a degree in biology and played competitive ice hockey. Her early career included research and healthcare investment roles, providing her with valuable insights into the complexities and inefficiencies of the healthcare industry.

## The Genesis of 23andMe: A Vision for Personalized Healthcare

Wojcicki's entrepreneurial journey was sparked by her frustration with the lack of personalized healthcare and preventive medicine. She envisioned a world where individuals could have direct access to their genetic information to make informed health decisions. In 2006, Wojcicki co-founded 23andMe with Linda Avey and Paul Cusenza. The company's mission was to provide affordable, direct-to-consumer genetic testing, enabling people to understand their genetic predispositions and take proactive steps in managing their health.

## Building 23andMe: Overcoming Initial Skepticism

Building 23andMe was fraught with challenges. The concept of personal genetic testing was revolutionary and met with significant skepticism from both the medical community and potential investors. Wojcicki faced the daunting task of convincing stakeholders of the value and safety of direct-to-consumer genetic testing. The company initially struggled to gain traction and secure funding. However, Wojcicki's determination and strategic thinking eventually paid off. She raised the necessary capital and assembled a team of experts in genetics, technology, and business.

The launch of 23andMe's Personal Genome Service in 2007 marked a significant milestone. For a relatively low cost, customers could mail in a saliva sample and receive detailed reports on their genetic traits, ancestry, and health risks. This democratization of genetic information was groundbreaking, offering consumers unprecedented insights into their health and heritage.

## Regulatory Hurdles: A Test of Resilience

Despite the initial excitement, 23andMe faced major regulatory challenges. In 2013, the FDA ordered the company to halt its health-related genetic tests, citing concerns about the accuracy and clinical validity of the information provided. This was a significant setback, threatening the company's future. Wojcicki and her team worked tirelessly to address the FDA's concerns, conducting rigorous validation studies and enhancing the quality of their reports.

Wojcicki's resilience and commitment to transparency paid off. In 2015, the FDA granted 23andMe authorization to market the first direct-to-consumer genetic test for carrier status. This milestone not only validated the company's scientific approach but also paved the way for expanded health reports. Wojcicki's ability to navigate complex regulatory landscapes and her unwavering belief in the company's mission were crucial to overcoming this adversity.

## Scaling and Expanding: Partnerships and Innovations

With regulatory hurdles largely behind them, 23andMe scaled rapidly. The company expanded its product offerings to include a range of health and ancestry reports, continuously improving the accuracy and depth of their genetic insights. Wojcicki's leadership was instrumental in forging partnerships with pharmaceutical companies and research institutions, leveraging 23andMe's vast genetic database for groundbreaking research.

One notable partnership was with GlaxoSmithKline (GSK) in 2018, which aimed to develop innovative treatments using genetic insights. This collaboration highlighted the potential of 23andMe's data to drive medical research and personalized medicine, aligning with Wojcicki's vision of transforming healthcare through genetics.

## IPO and Industry Impact: Pioneering Personal Genomics

In June 2021, 23andMe went public through a merger with a special purpose acquisition company (SPAC), marking a significant milestone for the company. The IPO underscored the growing acceptance and importance of genetic testing in healthcare. Wojcicki's leadership and vision had successfully positioned 23andMe as a leader in the personal genomics industry.

## Insights and Vision: Empowering Individuals with Genetic Information

Wojcicki's journey offers valuable lessons in resilience, innovation, and the importance of mission-driven leadership. "Our goal has always been to empower individuals with their own genetic information," Wojcicki explained in an interview. Her commitment to transparency, scientific rigor, and consumer empowerment has set 23andMe apart in a rapidly evolving industry.

"Believing in yourself has immeasurable value," says Wojcicki. When she launched 23andMe, she was met with skepticism from many, including high-profile geneticists. "It's helpful for people to realize the world is often wrong," she tells CNBC. Her mindset, influenced by her mother and her sisters, drove her to challenge societal norms and push forward despite naysayers.

## The Future of 23andMe: Advancing Healthcare Through Genetics

Looking ahead, Anne Wojcicki continues to drive 23andMe's growth and innovation. The company's vision extends beyond personal genetic testing to encompass broader healthcare applications, including drug development and personalized medicine. Wojcicki remains committed to leveraging genetic information to improve health outcomes and advance scientific research.

Her vision for the future includes expanding access to genetic testing globally, ensuring that more people can benefit from personalized health insights. Wojcicki also aims to deepen 23andMe's research efforts, contributing to a better understanding of the genetic basis of diseases and developing targeted therapies.

## A Commitment to Innovation and Education

Wojcicki also emphasizes the importance of integrating genetics into medical education and healthcare workflows. "Innovation requires pushing boundaries and navigating setbacks. The key is to stay focused on your mission and be willing to adapt and learn from challenges," she advises aspiring entrepreneurs. Collaborations with pharmaceutical companies and integrating genetics into medical school training are crucial for comprehensive patient care and the future of personalized medicine.

## Conclusion

Anne Wojcicki's journey serves as a powerful reminder that innovation often requires challenging the status quo and persevering through setbacks. Her story is an inspiring example of how a clear vision, coupled with resilience and dedication, can drive transformative change. As she continues to lead 23andMe into the future, Wojcicki's impact on the genomics industry and healthcare will undoubtedly be felt for generations to come.

# Ben Chestnut

## Turning Setbacks into Billions

Born in 1974 in Augusta, Georgia, Chestnut grew up in a modest household where his parents instilled the values of hard work and perseverance. His father was a postal worker, and his mother worked in a factory. Chestnut attended Georgia Institute of Technology, where he studied industrial design, a field that would later influence his approach to building products and businesses.

## Early Career and the Birth of Mailchimp

After graduating, Chestnut worked various jobs, including as a web designer. He co-founded a web design agency with Dan Kurzius called The Rocket Science Group. While their agency was doing well, they noticed a recurring problem among their clients: the need for an affordable and user-friendly email marketing tool. In 2001, Chestnut and Kurzius decided to pivot their business to address this gap, creating an email marketing service that would eventually become Mailchimp.

## The Story of His Firing and Comeback

In an unexpected turn of events, Chestnut faced a significant personal setback early in his career when he was let go from a web design job. This moment of adversity, however, became a catalyst for his entrepreneurial spirit. Rather than being deterred, Chestnut used this experience as a launching pad, co-founding The Rocket Science Group shortly thereafter. This venture eventually led to the birth of Mailchimp. His journey from being fired to creating a billion-dollar company is a testament to his resilience and ability to turn setbacks into opportunities.

## Bootstrapping Mailchimp

The early days of Mailchimp were challenging. Chestnut and Kurzius bootstrapped the company, funding it entirely from their web design business profits. They worked tirelessly, often putting in long hours and making significant personal sacrifices to keep the company afloat. Despite these challenges, they remained committed to their vision of creating a powerful yet accessible email marketing tool for small businesses.

Mailchimp's initial growth was slow, and Chestnut faced significant competition from larger, well-funded companies. However, his focus on simplicity, user experience, and customer support began to set Mailchimp apart. The company introduced a freemium model in 2009, allowing users to access basic features for free while paying for premium services. This model proved to be a game-changer, driving rapid user adoption and growth.

## Overcoming Adversity

Building Mailchimp was not without its setbacks. Chestnut had to navigate numerous challenges, including managing cash flow, scaling the business, and maintaining the company culture as they grew. One of the most significant challenges came during the 2008 financial crisis, which threatened the survival of many small businesses, including Mailchimp. Chestnut's leadership and adaptability were crucial during this period. He focused on understanding customer needs and continuously improving the product to provide more value.

## Achieving Success

Despite the challenges, Mailchimp continued to grow, driven by Chestnut's relentless focus on innovation and customer satisfaction. By 2015, Mailchimp had become one of the largest email marketing platforms in the world, serving millions of customers and generating hundreds of millions in revenue. The company's success was fueled by its commitment to empowering small businesses with the tools they needed to succeed in digital marketing.

In 2021, Mailchimp reached a significant milestone when Intuit acquired the company for $12 billion, marking one of the largest exits for a bootstrapped company in history.

Chestnut's leadership style, characterized by humility and a focus on long-term growth, played a significant role in Mailchimp's success. He prioritized building a supportive and inclusive company culture, ensuring that employees felt valued and motivated to contribute to the company's mission.

## Insights and Vision

Ben Chestnut's journey offers valuable insights into the importance of perseverance, customer focus, and innovation. "Success is about staying true to your mission and continuously finding ways to solve your customers' problems," Chestnut said in an interview. His commitment to understanding and addressing customer needs has been a cornerstone of Mailchimp's success.

Chestnut also emphasizes the importance of resilience and adaptability. "Building a business is a marathon, not a sprint. You have to be prepared for the ups and downs and stay focused on your long-term vision," he advises aspiring entrepreneurs. His ability to navigate challenges and remain dedicated to his mission has been key to his success.

## The Impact and Future of Mailchimp

Ben Chestnut's impact on the digital marketing industry is profound. By providing small businesses with affordable and effective email marketing tools, he has empowered countless entrepreneurs to grow their businesses and reach new customers. Mailchimp's success has also set a new standard for customer-centric product development and innovation in the tech industry.

## Conclusion

Ben Chestnut's journey from a modest upbringing and a career setback to leading one of the world's largest email marketing platforms is a testament to the power of resilience and innovation. His unwavering commitment to solving customer problems and his ability to turn adversity into opportunity have set new standards in tech entrepreneurship. Chestnut's story is an inspiring reminder that with determination, a clear vision, and a focus on customer needs, extraordinary success is possible. His legacy continues to influence and empower entrepreneurs worldwide, demonstrating that true innovation lies in the ability to adapt and persevere.

# Sophia Amoruso

## From Dumpster Diving to Building an Empire

Born in 1984 in San Diego, California, Sophia Amoruso grew up facing numerous challenges from an early age. Her parents divorced when she was young, and she struggled with ADHD, making her school years difficult. After dropping out of community college, Amoruso moved out and worked various odd jobs, from a Subway sandwich artist to a security guard. Her life took an unexpected turn when she started shoplifting and dumpster diving for survival.

## Vintage Dreams

Amoruso's entrepreneurial journey began in 2006 when she decided to turn her passion for vintage fashion into a business. With no formal training or experience in business, she started selling vintage clothes on eBay under the store name Nasty Gal Vintage. She meticulously curated her inventory, styled the clothes, and photographed them herself, creating a unique brand that resonated with young, fashion-forward women. Her knack for identifying and marketing unique pieces quickly set her apart from other sellers.

Nasty Gal's success wasn't immediate. Amoruso spent countless hours researching fashion trends, optimizing listings, and engaging with her customers. Her dedication paid off, and within a few years, Nasty Gal grew from a small eBay store to a thriving online retailer. By 2008, she had moved off eBay and launched her own website, Nasty Gal, which saw rapid growth and success.

## Growing Pains: Challenges in Scaling Nasty Gal

Despite the rapid growth, building Nasty Gal was not without its challenges. Amoruso faced significant obstacles, including managing cash flow, scaling operations, and maintaining the unique brand identity that had made Nasty Gal successful. As the company expanded, she had to learn quickly how to lead a growing team and navigate the complexities of running a larger business.

One of the most significant challenges came in 2016 when Nasty Gal filed for bankruptcy. The rapid expansion had led to financial difficulties, and the company struggled to compete with larger, more established retailers. Despite this setback, Amoruso remained resilient and focused on her next steps.

## Reinventing Success: The Birth of Girlboss

In 2014, before Nasty Gal's bankruptcy, Amoruso published her memoir, "#GIRLBOSS," which detailed her journey from misfit to CEO. The book became a New York Times bestseller and resonated with a generation of young women seeking inspiration and empowerment. The success of the book led to the creation of Girlboss Media, a platform dedicated to providing content, community, and resources for ambitious women.

Girlboss Media quickly gained traction, hosting conferences and creating content that inspired women to pursue their entrepreneurial dreams. Amoruso's ability to reinvent herself and leverage her experiences into a new venture demonstrated her resilience and adaptability.

## Shitty Jobs: The Unseen Side of Success

Before her success with Nasty Gal, Amoruso held various odd jobs that shaped her work ethic and determination. She scrubbed ring-around-the-collar off of men's shirts, worked in bookstores and record stores, and even watered lawns in business parks. These experiences, though often short-lived and challenging, taught her valuable lessons in perseverance and hard work.

## Unconventional Education: Learning Beyond the Classroom

Amoruso's relationship with education was complex. After a year of establishing residency in Washington State, she realized that a traditional degree might not be the key to her success. She took community college classes in photography and other subjects she was passionate about but ultimately decided to pursue her interests outside of a formal educational setting. This decision to follow her own path was pivotal in her journey.

## Insights and Vision: Authenticity and Resilience

Amoruso's journey offers valuable insights into the importance of resilience, adaptability, and staying true to one's vision. "Failure is not the end; it's a stepping stone to something greater," she stated in an interview. Her ability to turn setbacks into opportunities for growth and learning is a testament to her entrepreneurial spirit.

Amoruso also emphasizes the importance of authenticity and connecting with one's audience. "Building a brand is about creating something that people can relate to and believe in," she advises aspiring entrepreneurs. Her success with Nasty Gal and Girlboss is a reflection of her ability to create and market a brand that resonated deeply with her audience.

## Empowering Women: The Legacy of Girlboss

Sophia Amoruso's impact on the fashion and media industries is profound. Through Nasty Gal, she demonstrated the power of e-commerce and social media in building a successful brand. With Girlboss, she has created a platform that empowers and inspires women to pursue their passions and entrepreneurial dreams.

Looking ahead, Amoruso continues to drive the growth of Girlboss, exploring new ways to support and connect ambitious women. Her vision for Girlboss includes expanding its reach globally and creating more resources and opportunities for women to succeed in their careers and personal lives.

## Conclusion

Sophia Amoruso's journey from dumpster diving to building a fashion empire is a powerful testament to resilience, creativity, and authenticity. Her rise with Nasty Gal and subsequent reinvention with Girlboss highlight her ability to turn setbacks into opportunities. Amoruso's story inspires entrepreneurs to embrace their unique paths, maintain their authenticity, and see failures as stepping stones to greater success. By empowering women through her platforms and sharing her experiences, Amoruso continues to leave a lasting impact on the worlds of fashion and business, proving that with determination and vision, any challenge can be transformed into triumph.

# Adriana Gascoigne

## Bridging the Gender Gap in Tech

Born in 1980 in Napa Valley, California, Adriana Gascoigne grew up in a multicultural family with a Spanish immigrant father and a mother of Mexican and Japanese descent, who instilled in her values of hard work and resilience.

Gascoigne pursued her education at the University of California, Berkeley, earning a degree in Sociology. Upon graduation, she plunged into the tech industry, taking on roles in various Silicon Valley startups. Despite her qualifications and dedication, Gascoigne quickly encountered the harsh realities of a male-dominated field, facing gender bias, discrimination, and a lack of mentorship. This environment often left her feeling isolated and undervalued, experiences that would later fuel her passion for change.

## Turning Adversity into Advocacy

Gascoigne's pivotal moment came during a particularly challenging period at a startup where she was one of the few women on the team. Daily microaggressions and blatant sexism culminated in a confrontation with a male colleague who questioned her competence based on her gender. This incident ignited a determination in Gascoigne to create a more inclusive and supportive environment for women in tech.

## Lighting the Spark

In 2007, driven by her experiences and a desire to make a meaningful impact, Gascoigne founded Girls in Tech, a nonprofit organization dedicated to empowering women in technology and entrepreneurship. Starting with no initial funding and minimal resources, she organized events, workshops, and mentorship programs to support women in the tech industry. The early days were filled with adversity, including skepticism from potential sponsors and backlash from those who dismissed the need for gender diversity initiatives. Despite these challenges, Gascoigne's passion and perseverance kept her going, often using her own money to sustain the organization.

Today, Girls in Tech is recognized as one of the most influential and impactful nonprofit organizations in the United States, known for its significant social impact and successful initiatives.

## Rising Above the Storm

A dramatic moment in Gascoigne's journey came during the 2008 financial crisis. With funding for diversity initiatives becoming even harder to secure, Gascoigne faced the real possibility of shutting down Girls in Tech. In a bold move, she leveraged social media to raise awareness and support for her cause. The grassroots campaign she launched brought an overwhelming response, with women from around the world sharing their own stories of adversity and offering support. This outpouring of solidarity helped Gascoigne secure crucial partnerships and funding, allowing her to continue and expand the organization's efforts.

## Global Reach: Building a Movement

With renewed energy and resources, Girls in Tech began to grow. Gascoigne expanded the organization's reach by establishing chapters in cities around the world, each focused on providing local women with the tools, resources, and community needed to thrive in the tech industry. Initiatives like hackathons, coding boot camps, and leadership development programs empowered thousands of women to pursue careers in technology. One particularly impactful initiative was the Mentorship Program, which paired young women with experienced tech professionals, providing valuable guidance and support while building a strong network of women in tech.

## Changing the Game

Gascoigne's relentless efforts did not go unnoticed. Girls in Tech received numerous accolades and recognition from major tech companies, media outlets, and industry leaders. Gascoigne herself became a sought-after speaker and advisor, sharing her insights on gender diversity and inclusion at conferences and events worldwide. In 2016, she was invited to speak at the United Nations, highlighting the importance of gender equality in technology and the impact of Girls in Tech. This recognition validated her work and underscored the global relevance of her mission.

## Empowering a New Generation

Adriana Gascoigne's journey offers profound insights into the power of resilience, community, and advocacy. "Creating change requires courage and persistence," she often says. Her ability to turn personal adversity into a driving force for positive change has been a hallmark of her success. Gascoigne also emphasizes the importance of community and support. "We are stronger together. Building a network of support and mentorship is crucial for overcoming challenges and achieving success," she advises aspiring entrepreneurs and advocates.

## Envisioning an Inclusive Future

Looking ahead, Gascoigne remains committed to expanding the reach and impact of Girls in Tech. She envisions a future where gender diversity in tech is the norm, not the exception. To achieve this, she plans to introduce new programs focused on emerging technologies, entrepreneurship, and global collaboration. Gascoigne's vision extends beyond just increasing the number of women in tech; she aims to create a more inclusive and equitable tech industry where everyone, regardless of gender, can thrive and contribute.

## Conclusion

Adriana Gascoigne's journey exemplifies the profound impact of resilience, advocacy, and community in the tech industry. From her early challenges in Silicon Valley to founding a global movement with Girls in Tech, her path has been defined by courageous decisions and an unwavering dedication to empowering women in technology. Gascoigne's ability to transform personal adversities into opportunities for growth and change has not only enriched the lives of countless women but also established a new benchmark for inclusivity and support within the tech sector.

# Sam Altman

## The Visionary Behind OpenAI

Born in 1985 in St. Louis, Missouri, Sam Altman displayed a keen interest in technology from a young age. As a child, he was known for his curiosity and intelligence, often taking apart household electronics to understand how they worked. His passion for technology was evident early on, leading him to learn to program by the time he was 8 years old.

## From Stanford to Loopt: The Early Entrepreneurial Days

Sam Altman's entrepreneurial journey began in 2005 while he was still a student at Stanford University. Teaming up with a few classmates, Altman founded Loopt, a location-based social networking app. Loopt aimed to revolutionize how people interacted with their surroundings by allowing users to share their location with friends. Despite the initial excitement, Loopt didn't reach the monumental success the founders had hoped for. However, Altman's determination and innovative thinking led to a successful exit, selling Loopt for $43 million just a few years later.

## Rising Star at Y Combinator

Altman's success with Loopt caught the attention of Paul Graham, co-founder of the prestigious startup accelerator Y Combinator. Impressed by Altman's vision and entrepreneurial spirit, Graham hand-picked him to succeed him as the president of Y Combinator in 2014. During his five-year tenure, Altman played a pivotal role in bankrolling and nurturing some of the most important companies of our generation, including Airbnb, Reddit, and Instacart. His ability to spot potential and guide startups through their critical early stages helped shape the modern tech landscape.

## The OpenAI Revolution

After leaving Y Combinator in 2019, Altman embarked on a new venture that would push the boundaries of technology even further. He partnered with Elon Musk on a secret project called OpenAI, a nonprofit research lab dedicated to advancing artificial intelligence for the benefit of humanity. Altman's passion for AI and his leadership skills propelled OpenAI to the forefront of AI research.

In a pivotal move, Altman and Musk introduced ChatGPT, an AI-powered chatbot. The launch of ChatGPT was nothing short of spectacular, attracting over a million users within just five days. This breakthrough demonstrated the incredible potential of artificial intelligence to engage and assist people in new and meaningful ways.

## A Bold Move: The Birth of OpenAI LP

Recognizing the enormous potential of ChatGPT and the need for substantial funding to continue its development, Altman made a strategic decision that would redefine OpenAI's future. He created a for-profit arm of the company called OpenAI LP. This restructuring allowed OpenAI to attract significant investment and operate with greater flexibility. In one of the boldest moves in corporate history, Altman secured a $10 billion investment from Microsoft. This partnership transformed OpenAI into a $40 billion powerhouse, positioning it as a leader in the AI industry.

## The Dramatic Firing and Triumphant Return

In a shocking turn of events, on November 17, 2023, OpenAI's board unexpectedly fired Sam Altman from his position as CEO. The reasons cited included a lack of trust and accusations of toxic leadership, as well as undisclosed ownership of the OpenAI Startup Fund. The firing caused significant turmoil within the company, leading to internal chaos and a swift push from employees and key stakeholders, including Microsoft, for Altman's reinstatement. Within days, Altman returned as CEO, backed by overwhelming support from employees and partners. His return marked a renewed focus on OpenAI's mission and highlighted his indispensable role in the company's vision.

## Reflections and Vision

Altman's journey is a testament to his ability to foresee and shape the future of technology. "Innovation is not just about having a great idea; it's about being able to see where the world is heading and positioning yourself to meet future needs," Altman explained in an interview. His knack for identifying trends and willingness to take calculated risks have been instrumental in his success.

Altman also underscores the importance of mentorship and a strong support network. "I've been incredibly fortunate to have mentors like Paul Graham who believed in me and gave me opportunities to grow.

Surround yourself with people who challenge and inspire you," he advises aspiring entrepreneurs.

## The Impact and Future of OpenAI

The impact of Altman's work with OpenAI is profound. ChatGPT and other AI innovations developed under his leadership have the potential to revolutionize industries from healthcare to education to customer service. Altman's vision for OpenAI is to continue pushing the boundaries of what AI can achieve while ensuring that these advancements benefit all of humanity.

## Conclusion:

Sam Altman's story is a powerful example of visionary leadership and relentless innovation. From his early days with Loopt to transforming OpenAI into a global AI leader, Altman's journey is marked by bold decisions and a deep understanding of the future of technology. His ability to inspire and drive change serves as a beacon for entrepreneurs and innovators worldwide. Altman's commitment to ethical AI development and his ability to navigate complex challenges ensure that his impact on technology and society will be felt for generations to come.

# Stewart Butterfield

## From Failed Game to Billion-Dollar Communication Platform

Born in 1973 in Lund, British Columbia, Stewart Butterfield grew up in a family of academics and social activists. His father, David Butterfield, was a prominent economist, and his mother, Norma Edelstein, a talented artist. This intellectually stimulating environment fostered his curiosity and creativity from an early age. Butterfield attended the University of Victoria, where he earned a degree in philosophy before completing a master's degree at the University of Cambridge.

## From Virtual Worlds to Photo Sharing

In 2002, Butterfield and his then-wife, Caterina Fake, co-founded Ludicorp, initially intended to develop an online game called Game Neverending. However, the game failed to gain traction, leading Butterfield to pivot to a different idea. Leveraging the photo-sharing capabilities built into the game, they launched Flickr in 2004. Flickr quickly became one of the most popular photo-sharing sites on the internet, pioneering social photo sharing with features like tagging and user comments. The platform's success caught the attention of Yahoo!, which acquired Flickr for $35 million in 2005.

Despite the financial success, the Yahoo! acquisition was bittersweet. Butterfield faced significant challenges integrating Flickr into Yahoo!'s corporate structure, leading to creative and operational frustrations. This experience taught him valuable lessons about corporate culture and the importance of maintaining a clear vision.

## Gaming Dreams and New Ventures

Undeterred by the mixed experience at Yahoo!, Butterfield set his sights on another ambitious project. In 2009, he co-founded Tiny Speck with the goal of creating Glitch, a highly imaginative, massively multiplayer online game. Glitch was a bold, creative endeavor that aimed to combine the whimsical elements of a child's imagination with complex social interactions. Despite its innovative design and a passionate user base, Glitch struggled to attract a mainstream audience and generate sufficient revenue.

In 2012, after years of development and significant investment, Butterfield made the difficult decision to shut down Glitch. The closure was a heartbreaking setback, not just financially, but emotionally as well. The team at Tiny Speck had poured their hearts into the project, and its failure was a significant blow. Yet, this failure would lay the groundwork for one of the most successful pivots in tech history.

## The Birth of Slack

During the development of Glitch, Butterfield and his team created an internal communication tool to help them collaborate more effectively. Recognizing the potential of this tool, they decided to pivot once again and transform it into a standalone product. In 2013, Slack was born, revolutionizing workplace communication by offering a seamless, intuitive platform that integrated with a variety of other services.

The early days of Slack were filled with uncertainty. Butterfield faced the daunting challenge of convincing businesses to adopt a new communication tool in a crowded market dominated by established players like Microsoft and Google. Despite these challenges, Butterfield's vision for a more efficient and enjoyable workplace communication experience resonated with early adopters.

## Surpassing Expectations

Slack's growth was nothing short of meteoric. Within a year of its launch, Slack had over 120,000 daily active users. The platform's success was driven by its ability to solve real problems for teams and businesses, offering features that enhanced productivity and collaboration. Butterfield's emphasis on creating a delightful user experience set Slack apart from its competitors.

One dramatic moment in Slack's journey came when it experienced a major outage in 2015. The platform went down for several hours, causing significant disruption for its users. Butterfield's response was a masterclass in crisis management. He and his team communicated transparently with users, quickly addressing the issue and reinforcing their commitment to reliability. This incident not only highlighted the importance of trust but also strengthened Slack's relationship with its user base.

## Transforming Workplace Communication

In June 2019, Slack went public through a direct listing on the New York Stock Exchange, eschewing the traditional IPO route. This move reflected Butterfield's unconventional approach and confidence in the company's value. The direct listing was a resounding success, with Slack's valuation soaring to over $20 billion. This milestone underscored Slack's position as a leading communication platform and validated Butterfield's vision.

Butterfield's leadership and innovative spirit have had a profound impact on the tech industry. Slack has transformed how teams communicate and collaborate, setting new standards for workplace efficiency and integration. The platform's success has also inspired a wave of new startups focused on improving workplace productivity.

## Philosophical Foundations

Stewart Butterfield's journey offers valuable insights into the importance of resilience, adaptability, and staying true to one's vision. "Failure is not the end; it's an opportunity to learn and grow," Butterfield often emphasizes. His ability to pivot from failures and recognize new opportunities has been a hallmark of his success.

Butterfield also stresses the importance of creating products that delight users. "The best products are those that people love to use every day," he advises. His focus on user experience and customer satisfaction has been a key driver of Slack's success.

## The Future of Slack and Beyond

Looking ahead, Butterfield continues to drive Slack's growth and innovation. He remains committed to expanding Slack's capabilities and exploring new ways to enhance workplace communication. His vision for Slack includes deeper integrations with other business tools and leveraging artificial intelligence to provide even more personalized and efficient communication solutions.

Butterfield's journey is far from over. His ability to navigate challenges and seize new opportunities suggests that he will continue to be a transformative force in the tech industry.

## Conclusion

Stewart Butterfield's story is a powerful example of how resilience, creativity, and a commitment to innovation can lead to extraordinary success. From the early days of Flickr to the dramatic failure of Glitch and the meteoric rise of Slack, Butterfield's journey is marked by bold decisions and an unwavering dedication to creating products that solve real problems. His ability to turn setbacks into opportunities for growth and innovation has revolutionized workplace communication and set a new standard for what is possible in tech entrepreneurship

# Eileen Fisher

## Crafting a Timeless Fashion Legacy

Born in Des Plaines, Illinois, in 1950, Fisher grew up in a working-class family. She attended the University of Illinois at Urbana-Champaign, initially studying home economics before switching to interior design. Fisher's early career took her to New York City, where she worked as an interior and graphic designer. Despite her success, she felt unfulfilled and began to seek a new path that aligned more closely with her passions.

## Inspiration from the East

The pivotal moment for Fisher came during a trip to Japan in the early 1980s. She was struck by the simplicity and elegance of Japanese clothing, which contrasted sharply with the fast-paced, trend-driven fashion industry in the United States. Inspired by the minimalist aesthetic and the versatility of the garments she saw, Fisher conceived an idea for a clothing line that emphasized simplicity, comfort, and timeless style.

With no formal training in fashion design and limited business experience, Fisher faced significant skepticism from friends and potential investors. Despite these doubts, she was determined to bring her vision to life. She sketched her first designs and began to explore fabric options, focusing on natural materials that felt good against the skin and draped beautifully.

## Launching a Dream with $350

In 1984, with $350 in savings, Fisher launched her eponymous fashion brand, Eileen Fisher Inc. She started by creating a small collection of four basic pieces: a box-top, a tunic, a pair of pants, and a kimono jacket. These pieces were designed to be mixed and matched, offering versatility and ease to women's wardrobes.

Fisher faced immediate challenges. As an unknown designer with no retail presence, she struggled to get her collection into stores. She personally visited boutiques and department stores, pitching her minimalist designs to skeptical buyers. Her breakthrough came when a small New York boutique agreed to carry her collection, which sold out quickly. This initial success validated her vision and gave her the confidence to continue.

## The Road Less Traveled

Building her brand was far from easy. Fisher faced financial constraints and the constant pressure to prove that her minimalist, timeless designs could compete in a trend-driven industry. One of the most dramatic moments in her early career came when she ran out of funds to produce her next collection. In a bold move, Fisher decided to take out a personal loan, risking her financial security to keep the business afloat.

Fisher's commitment to quality and sustainability also set her apart but presented significant challenges. She insisted on using high-quality, sustainable fabrics, which were more expensive and harder to source.

This decision initially limited her production capabilities and strained her budget. Despite these obstacles, Fisher remained steadfast in her vision, believing that her customers would appreciate and value the integrity of her designs.

## Innovating with Purpose

As Eileen Fisher Inc. grew, Fisher continued to innovate and expand her product offerings. She introduced new designs and experimented with different fabrics while staying true to her core principles of simplicity, comfort, and timelessness. Her focus on sustainability became a defining feature of the brand. Fisher implemented practices such as using organic cotton, linen, and wool, and promoting fair labor practices.

One particularly innovative initiative was the Renew program, which encouraged customers to return their old Eileen Fisher garments in exchange for store credit. These garments were then resold or repurposed, aligning with Fisher's commitment to sustainability and reducing waste. This program not only reinforced the brand's values but also built a loyal customer base that appreciated the company's ethical stance.

## Transforming Setbacks into Opportunities

Fisher's dedication to her vision and values earned her widespread recognition. Eileen Fisher Inc. became a beacon for sustainable and ethical fashion, influencing other brands to adopt similar practices. Fisher herself received numerous accolades, including being named one of Time magazine's 100 most influential people.

In 2009, Fisher took a significant step to secure the future of her brand by establishing the Eileen Fisher Leadership Institute. This program aimed to inspire young women to become leaders and changemakers, reflecting Fisher's belief in the power of mentorship and community.

## Leading by Example

Eileen Fisher's journey offers profound insights into the importance of staying true to one's values, resilience, and the impact of sustainable practices. "Success is not just about growth; it's about doing the right thing for people and the planet," Fisher often says. Her unwavering commitment to sustainability and ethical practices has set a new standard in the fashion industry.

Fisher also emphasizes the importance of simplicity and authenticity. "Creating something timeless means focusing on what truly matters and eliminating the unnecessary," she advises aspiring entrepreneurs. Her ability to maintain a clear vision and adapt to challenges has been key to her enduring success.

## Empowering Future Generations

Looking ahead, Fisher remains dedicated to driving her brand's growth while deepening its commitment to sustainability. She continues to explore innovative ways to reduce the environmental impact of fashion, from developing new eco-friendly fabrics to enhancing the company's recycling programs. Her vision for the future includes expanding the Renew program and increasing transparency in the supply chain.

Fisher's influence extends beyond her brand. She actively advocates for sustainable practices in the fashion industry and supports initiatives that promote ethical manufacturing and fair labor practices. Her legacy is one of integrity, innovation, and a steadfast commitment to making a positive impact.

## Embracing the Future

Eileen Fisher's story is a powerful example of how a clear vision, resilience, and commitment to values can lead to extraordinary success. From her early days as a designer with no formal training to building a globally recognized brand, Fisher's journey is marked by bold decisions and an unwavering dedication to simplicity and sustainability. Her ability to turn challenges into opportunities for growth and innovation has revolutionized the fashion industry and set a new standard for ethical business practices. Fisher's journey serves as an inspiring reminder that with passion, perseverance, and a commitment to doing what's right, any obstacle can be overcome.

## Conclusion

Eileen Fisher's journey is a testament to the power of staying true to one's values and continuously seeking opportunities for innovation and growth. Her story exemplifies how a clear vision and commitment to ethical practices can lead to lasting success and influence. Fisher's legacy in the fashion industry is marked by her dedication to sustainability and her ability to inspire change, making her an enduring figure in ethical business practices.

# Tristan Walker

## Shaping the Future of Grooming and Healthcare

Born in Queens, New York, in 1984, Tristan Walker faced significant hardships growing up. His father was murdered when Walker was just three years old, leaving his mother to raise him and his brother alone in a rough neighborhood. Despite these adversities, Walker's mother instilled in him the values of hard work and education, which fueled his drive to succeed.

## Transforming Adversity into Opportunity

Walker attended the prestigious Hotchkiss School on a scholarship, an opportunity that opened doors to a brighter future. He went on to earn a degree in economics from Stony Brook University and later an MBA from Stanford University. During his time at Stanford, Walker interned at Twitter and later joined the early team at Foursquare, where he played a crucial role in the company's growth and business development.

Despite his success at Foursquare, Walker experienced firsthand the lack of diversity in Silicon Valley. He often found himself as the only person of color in the room, an experience that ignited his passion for creating opportunities for underrepresented minorities in the tech industry.

## Recognizing a Gap in the Market

Walker's entrepreneurial journey began with a personal frustration: finding suitable grooming products for BIPOC men. He noticed that mainstream grooming products were not designed with the specific needs of BIPOC men in mind, leading to issues like razor bumps and skin irritation. Recognizing a significant gap in the market, Walker saw an opportunity to create a brand that catered specifically to the grooming needs of men of color.

## Building Walker & Company Brands

In 2013, Walker founded Walker & Company Brands with the mission to make health and beauty simple for the BIPOC community. The company's flagship product, Bevel, is a shaving system designed to prevent razor bumps and irritation. With no prior experience in product development, Walker faced significant challenges in bringing Bevel to market. He invested his savings and raised capital from investors who believed in his vision, despite the skepticism of others who doubted the market potential.

One of the most dramatic moments in Walker's journey came when he decided to go all-in on his startup. He and his wife sold their house and moved into a smaller apartment to fund the business. This bold move demonstrated his unwavering commitment to his vision, even in the face of uncertainty.

## Surmounting Challenges with Perseverance

Building Walker & Company was fraught with challenges. Walker faced difficulties in securing manufacturing partners who could meet the high standards he set for Bevel. He also had to educate investors and retailers about the unique needs of his target market, often encountering skepticism and bias.

Despite these obstacles, Walker's determination and strategic thinking paid off. He focused on building a strong brand and creating a community around Bevel. His efforts to connect directly with customers through social media and other channels helped build a loyal following.

## Achieving Market Success

Bevel launched to critical acclaim and quickly gained traction among consumers. The company's commitment to quality and addressing the specific needs of the BIPOC community resonated with its audience. By 2018, Walker & Company had expanded its product line and distribution, reaching a wider market and solidifying its position as a leader in the grooming industry.

In a significant milestone, Walker & Company was acquired by Procter & Gamble in 2018. According to reports, Proctor and Gamble could have paid anywhere between $20 million and $40 million for the company. The acquisition provided the resources and infrastructure needed to scale the business while allowing Walker to continue leading the company and pursuing its mission. This partnership marked a major achievement and validated Walker's vision and hard work.

## Valuable Insights and Forward Vision

Tristan Walker's journey offers valuable insights into the importance of resilience, customer focus, and addressing underserved markets. "Success comes from understanding the unique needs of your customers and delivering products that truly serve them," Walker often emphasizes. His ability to identify and address a significant market gap has been key to his success.

Walker also stresses the importance of perseverance and strategic risk-taking. "Building a business requires bold decisions and a willingness to take risks. You have to be all-in and committed to your vision," he advises aspiring entrepreneurs. His journey reflects the power of dedication and the impact of creating products that meet real needs.

## Future Endeavors and Continuing Impact

Looking ahead, Walker remains committed to expanding Walker & Company's impact. He envisions further growth and innovation in the grooming and healthcare industries, continuing to address the specific needs of his community. His focus includes developing new products and exploring opportunities to enhance overall health and wellness for his target market.

Walker's influence extends beyond his company. He actively advocates for diversity and inclusion in the tech and business communities, supporting initiatives that create opportunities for underrepresented communities. His work has inspired a new generation of entrepreneurs to pursue their visions and challenge industry norms.

## Conclusion

Tristan Walker's journey from the streets of Queens to the boardrooms of Silicon Valley is a testament to the power of resilience, innovation, and unwavering commitment to a vision. His story is not just one of personal success but a beacon of inspiration for aspiring entrepreneurs everywhere. Walker's ability to transform personal adversity into a thriving business that addresses the unique needs of the BIPOC community is a reminder that true innovation often stems from deeply personal experiences and a desire to make a meaningful impact.

# Tope Awotona

## Scheduling Success Through Adversity

Born in Lagos, Nigeria, in 1981, Awotona faced significant challenges from a young age. Growing up in a turbulent environment, he witnessed the tragic death of his father, who was killed during a carjacking when Awotona was just 12 years old. This traumatic event had a profound impact on him, instilling a sense of urgency and a drive to succeed. In 1996, Awotona moved to the United States with his family, seeking better opportunities and a safer environment. He attended the University of Georgia, where he studied computer science before switching to business and management information systems. Despite the hardships, Awotona remained focused on his education and career aspirations.

## The Early Hustle

After graduating, Awotona worked in sales at various tech companies, including IBM and Dell. While he gained valuable experience, he often felt unfulfilled and yearned to create something of his own. His entrepreneurial spirit led him to start several ventures, including a floral business and an e-commerce site selling projectors. Despite his efforts, these early businesses did not achieve significant success, but they provided valuable lessons in resilience and business management. He realized the importance of finding a problem he was passionate about solving rather than just focusing on making money.

## A Moment of Frustration Sparks Innovation

The idea for Calendly was born out of Awotona's personal frustration with scheduling meetings. He found the process of coordinating meeting times through endless back-and-forth emails to be inefficient and time-consuming. Realizing that many others shared this frustration, he saw an opportunity to create a solution that would simplify scheduling for everyone. In 2013, Awotona decided to invest his life savings, pulled from his 401k, and maxed out his credit cards to develop Calendly. With no technical co-founder and limited resources, he faced an uphill battle, hiring a team of contractors to bring his vision to life.

## Risking It All

The early days of Calendly were filled with challenges. Awotona faced skepticism from potential investors who doubted the viability of yet another scheduling tool in a crowded market. He also struggled to manage cash flow and ensure the product met his high standards for user experience and functionality. One of the most dramatic moments in Calendly's early journey came when Awotona ran out of money before the product was fully developed. Undeterred, he used his credit cards to fund the remaining development costs, demonstrating his unwavering commitment to the project. His perseverance paid off when Calendly launched to positive feedback and began gaining traction among users.

## The Grind Behind the Glamour

Despite the initial success, scaling Calendly was not without its obstacles. Awotona faced intense competition from established players in the scheduling and productivity space. He also had to navigate the complexities of growing a tech company, including hiring the right talent, managing a remote team, and continuously improving the product to meet user needs. Awotona's focus on customer feedback and his relentless pursuit of excellence set Calendly apart. He invested heavily in understanding user pain points and iterating on the product to enhance its features and usability. This customer-centric approach helped Calendly build a loyal user base and expand its reach.

## Turning Skeptics into Believers

Calendly's growth was exponential. By 2017, the platform had millions of users and was being used by individuals and businesses around the world to streamline their scheduling processes. The product's simplicity, reliability, and user-friendly interface resonated with users, driving widespread adoption. In 2021, Calendly achieved unicorn status with a valuation of over $3 billion, following a $350 million investment round led by OpenView Venture Partners and Iconiq Capital. This milestone validated Awotona's vision and the impact of Calendly in transforming how people schedule meetings. Today, Calendly has over 20 million users worldwide and is valued at over $1 billion. Awotona's journey from bootstrapping the company to achieving such heights underscores his determination and strategic focus.

## The Road to Unicorn Status

Tope Awotona's journey offers profound insights into the power of resilience, customer focus, and perseverance. "Success is about solving real problems and staying committed to your vision, even when faced with adversity," Awotona often emphasizes. His ability to turn personal frustration into a successful business highlights the importance of identifying and addressing market needs. Awotona also stresses the value of listening to customers. "Our users are our best source of feedback and inspiration. Continuously improving based on their needs is key to our success," he advises aspiring entrepreneurs. His dedication to creating a product that truly serves its users has been instrumental in Calendly's growth.

## Vision Beyond the Calendar

Looking ahead, Awotona remains committed to driving Calendly's growth and innovation. He envisions expanding the platform's capabilities to further simplify scheduling and enhance productivity for individuals and organizations. His focus includes integrating Calendly with more tools and platforms, leveraging artificial intelligence to provide smarter scheduling solutions, and expanding globally. Awotona's impact extends beyond Calendly. He actively supports initiatives that promote entrepreneurship and diversity in tech, reflecting his belief in the power of innovation and inclusion to drive positive change.

## Conclusion

Tope Awotona's legacy is not just in the success of Calendly but in his inspiring example of turning challenges into opportunities. His journey reminds us that with passion, perseverance, and a customer-centric approach, even the most daunting obstacles can be transformed into stepping stones toward extraordinary success.

Beyond his business acumen, Awotona's story is one of unwavering belief in his vision and the willingness to take bold risks. His journey from Lagos to becoming one of the few Black tech billionaires in the world underscores the importance of diversity and inclusion in driving innovation and positive change.

# Jennifer Hyman

## Revolutionizing Fashion with Rent the Runway

Born in New Rochelle, New York, in 1980, Jenn Hyman grew up in a supportive family that valued education and ambition. She attended Harvard University, where she majored in social studies. After graduating, she worked in various roles, including at Starwood Hotels and Resorts and at IMG, where she honed her skills in marketing and strategy. One of the most important lessons she learned early in her career was the value of being likable, which she discovered while interning at Starwood Hotels and Resorts. This lesson proved invaluable when she later founded Rent the Runway and needed to persuade designers and investors to believe in her vision.

## A Dress Dilemma That Sparked a Revolution

The idea for Rent the Runway was sparked by a personal experience in 2008. Hyman's sister faced a dilemma familiar to many women: she needed a stunning dress for a special event but couldn't justify the expense of buying one. This conversation led Hyman to recognize a significant gap in the market. Women wanted access to high-end fashion without the commitment of purchasing expensive garments they might only wear once. Hyman shared her idea with Jennifer Fleiss, a fellow Harvard Business School student. Together, they envisioned a company that would allow women to rent designer dresses for a fraction of the retail price, making fashion accessible and sustainable.

## From Concept to Couture

In 2009, Hyman and Fleiss founded Rent the Runway, starting with a small inventory of designer dresses and an ambitious vision. They faced immediate challenges, including skepticism from designers and investors who doubted that women would rent dresses. Hyman and Fleiss persevered, conducting extensive market research and refining their business model. One of the most dramatic moments in the early days came when they hosted a pop-up shop at Harvard, validating their concept and helping them secure initial funding and partnerships with designers.

## Turning Fashion Faux Pas into Fashion Triumphs

Building Rent the Runway was far from easy. Hyman and Fleiss faced significant logistical and operational challenges, from managing inventory to ensuring timely deliveries. They also had to navigate the complexities of building a technology platform that could handle reservations, payments, and customer service. One particularly challenging period came when they struggled with customer returns and garment damage. Determined to maintain high standards, Hyman implemented rigorous quality control measures and invested in a state-of-the-art dry cleaning facility. This commitment to excellence helped build trust with customers and designers alike.

## A Closet Full of Success: Hitting It Big

Rent the Runway's growth was rapid and transformative. The company introduced subscription services, allowing customers to rent multiple items for a monthly fee. This model proved to be incredibly popular, driving subscriber growth and recurring revenue. In 2019, Rent the Runway achieved unicorn status, with a valuation exceeding $1 billion. This milestone was a testament to Hyman's vision and leadership. The company's success also underscored the growing trend towards sustainable fashion, as more consumers sought alternatives to traditional retail.

## Navigating the Pandemic: A Second Founding Moment

The COVID-19 pandemic brought unprecedented challenges to Rent the Runway, described by Hyman as the "second founding moment" for the company. The pandemic forced Rent the Runway to make deep cuts and conduct layoffs to sustain through the business disruptions. However, Hyman saw this period as an opportunity for reinvention. She believed that the post-COVID era would shift towards smarter and more sustainable consumption patterns, making Rent the Runway more relevant than ever. The company widened its value proposition by offering renting, subscribing, or buying second-hand options, embracing the circular economy. Hyman envisioned a "living closet" concept, providing consumers with flexibility in usage length, promoting sustainability and smarter consumption.

## Visionary Leadership and Customer Connection

Jenn Hyman's journey offers valuable insights into the importance of resilience, customer focus, and the willingness to challenge industry norms. "Innovation is about solving real problems and creating value for your customers," Hyman often emphasizes. Her ability to identify a market gap and build a solution that resonated with consumers has been key to Rent the Runway's success. Hyman also highlights the importance of perseverance and adaptability. "The path to success is rarely a straight line. You have to be prepared to navigate challenges and pivot when necessary," she advises aspiring entrepreneurs.

## Future Threads

Looking ahead, Hyman remains committed to expanding Rent the Runway's impact and reach. She envisions further growth and innovation, including expanding the company's product offerings and exploring new markets. Her focus includes leveraging data and technology to enhance the customer experience and drive sustainability in the fashion industry. Hyman's influence extends beyond Rent the Runway. She actively advocates for gender equality and diversity in the workplace, supporting initiatives that promote female entrepreneurship and leadership. Her work has inspired a new generation of women to pursue their entrepreneurial dreams and challenge industry norms.

## Conclusion

Jennifer Hyman's journey with Rent the Runway is a testament to visionary leadership, innovation, and the power of resilience. From the initial spark of an idea inspired by her sister's dress dilemma to navigating the complexities of building a fashion-tech company, Hyman's story is marked by bold decisions and unwavering dedication. She transformed a simple concept into a billion-dollar business that not only revolutionized the fashion industry but also advocated for sustainable consumption.

Her story underscores the importance of perseverance, customer focus, and the courage to challenge industry norms. Jennifer Hyman's journey serves as an inspiring reminder that with determination, creativity, and a clear vision, it is possible to overcome any obstacle and achieve extraordinary success.

# Payal Kadakia

## Dancing Her Way to Disruptive Innovation

Born in New Jersey to Indian immigrant parents, Payal Kadakia was introduced to dance at a young age. She trained in classical Indian dance, which became a central part of her life and identity. Despite facing racial discrimination at school, her passion for dance provided her with an anchor and a sense of belonging. Kadakia attended MIT, where she studied operations research and economics, balancing her rigorous academic schedule with her love for dance. At MIT, she founded the university's first Indian dance company, MIT Chamak, which later inspired her to create Sa Dance, a platform for Indian American identity through movement .

## From Frustration to Fortune

Kadakia's career started at Bain & Company and Warner Music Group, where she gained valuable experience in strategy and business development. Despite her corporate success, she felt unfulfilled and longed to integrate her passion for dance with her professional life. In 2010, after a frustrating search for a dance class in New York City, Kadakia realized there was a significant gap in the market: people needed an easier way to discover and book fitness classes.

## Turning Failures into Features

In 2011, driven by her personal frustration and a desire to make fitness more accessible, Kadakia founded Classivity, which later rebranded as ClassPass. The initial concept was a search engine for fitness classes, but it struggled to gain traction. Undeterred, Kadakia and her team pivoted, launching a subscription-based model in 2013 that allowed users to take a variety of fitness classes at different studios for a flat monthly fee. This innovative approach quickly resonated with consumers, offering flexibility and variety that traditional gym memberships lacked.

## Dancing Around Doubters

Building ClassPass was fraught with challenges. Kadakia faced significant skepticism from investors who doubted the viability of her business model. Early fundraising efforts were met with rejection, and Kadakia had to navigate the complexities of building partnerships with fitness studios. One of the most dramatic moments came when the initial version of Classivity failed to attract users, forcing Kadakia to make the tough decision to pivot or shut down. She chose to pivot, demonstrating her resilience and adaptability.

Kadakia's breakthrough came when she realized the power of offering unlimited access to fitness classes for a monthly fee. This bold move transformed ClassPass from a struggling startup into a thriving business. Despite the financial risks and operational challenges, Kadakia's determination to create a user-centric product paid off. ClassPass quickly gained traction, and word-of-mouth referrals helped accelerate its growth.

## Leaping to Unicorn Status

ClassPass's growth was rapid and transformative. By 2014, the company had expanded to multiple cities, attracting thousands of users who valued the flexibility and variety it offered. Kadakia's focus on customer experience and her commitment to innovation helped build a loyal user base and establish ClassPass as a leader in the fitness industry.

In 2020, ClassPass achieved unicorn status with a valuation exceeding $1 billion, following a significant investment round. This milestone validated Kadakia's vision and highlighted the impact of her innovative approach to fitness. ClassPass's success also underscored the growing demand for flexible, on-demand fitness solutions, particularly among urban professionals.

## Mastering the Art of the Pivot

Payal Kadakia's journey offers valuable insights into the power of resilience, innovation, and customer focus. "Success comes from solving real problems and staying true to your mission," Kadakia often emphasizes. Her ability to pivot and adapt in response to market feedback has been key to ClassPass's success.

Kadakia also highlights the importance of perseverance and passion. "Building a business requires a deep connection to your purpose and a willingness to overcome obstacles," she advises aspiring entrepreneurs. Her journey reflects the power of following one's passion and the impact of creating products that genuinely enhance people's lives.

## Beyond the Barre

Looking ahead, Kadakia remains committed to driving ClassPass's growth and innovation. She envisions expanding the platform's capabilities to offer more personalized fitness experiences and exploring new markets globally. Her focus includes leveraging technology and data to enhance user experience and provide even more value to customers.

Kadakia's influence extends beyond ClassPass. She actively supports initiatives that promote entrepreneurship, particularly among women and minorities. Her work has inspired a new generation of entrepreneurs to pursue their passions and challenge industry norms.

## Conclusion

Payal Kadakia's journey is a vibrant dance of resilience, innovation, and unwavering dedication. From her childhood love of dance to the founding of ClassPass, Kadakia has consistently turned passion into purpose, transforming the fitness industry along the way. Her story highlights the importance of perseverance and the ability to pivot in the face of challenges. As ClassPass continues to grow and evolve, Kadakia's vision of making fitness accessible and enjoyable for all remains at the heart of the company's mission.

Kadakia's legacy is not just in the thriving business she built, but in the inspiration she provides to future entrepreneurs and dreamers, proving that one can indeed dance through life's challenges and emerge victorious.

# Travis Kalanick

## Navigating the Ride of a Lifetime

Born in Los Angeles, California, in 1976, Kalanick grew up in a middle-class family. His father was a civil engineer, and his mother was a retail advertiser. Kalanick displayed an early talent for math and computers, which he nurtured through his schooling. He attended the University of California, Los Angeles (UCLA), where he studied computer engineering, but dropped out to pursue his entrepreneurial ambitions.

## Paris Inspiration Ignites a Revolution

Kalanick's entrepreneurial journey began with Scour, a peer-to-peer search engine, and Red Swoosh, a content delivery network. Both ventures faced significant challenges: Scour ended in a lawsuit from major media companies, and Red Swoosh struggled to find its footing before being sold to Akamai Technologies in 2007. Despite these setbacks, Kalanick's experiences provided valuable lessons in resilience and innovation.

The pivotal moment for Kalanick came in 2008 when he attended a tech conference in Paris. Frustrated by the difficulty of finding a cab, he envisioned a simple solution: a service that allowed users to book a ride from their smartphone. This idea led to the creation of UberCab, which he co-founded with Garrett Camp in 2009. The concept was simple yet revolutionary: a ride-hailing service that connected passengers with drivers through a mobile app.

## Scaling Heights with Relentless Ambition

In 2010, Kalanick and Camp launched UberCab in San Francisco. The early days were marked by intense challenges, including regulatory hurdles and competition from traditional taxi services. The company faced a cease-and-desist order from the San Francisco Municipal Transportation Agency (SFMTA), which claimed that UberCab was operating as an unlicensed taxi service. This legal battle set the tone for Uber's aggressive expansion strategy, where Kalanick frequently clashed with regulators and competitors.

One of the most dramatic moments in Uber's early history was during the launch phase when Kalanick took to the streets himself to promote the service. He would approach potential riders, explaining the convenience and efficiency of Uber, often working late into the night. His hands-on approach and relentless drive were crucial in building Uber's initial user base and overcoming early skepticism.

## Overcoming Adversity and Scaling

As Uber began to gain traction in San Francisco, Kalanick faced the challenge of scaling the service to other cities. This required navigating a patchwork of local regulations and fierce opposition from the taxi industry. Kalanick's strategy was to move fast and establish a foothold before regulators could react. This approach, while controversial, proved effective in rapidly expanding Uber's presence across the

United States and internationally.

Kalanick's leadership style was characterized by his aggressive, no-holds-barred approach. He fostered a culture of relentless ambition and innovation at Uber, encouraging his team to "always be hustlin.'" This culture, while driving rapid growth and technological advancements, also led to significant internal and external conflicts.

## Navigating Success Through Stormy Waters

By 2014, Uber had expanded to numerous cities worldwide and was valued at billions of dollars. The company's success was driven by its ability to provide a convenient, cost-effective alternative to traditional taxi services. However, this success came with considerable controversy. Kalanick's aggressive tactics and confrontational approach often put Uber at odds with regulators, competitors, and even its own employees.

One particularly intense period came in 2017, known as "The Year of the Scandal." Uber faced a series of high-profile controversies, including allegations of workplace harassment, a toxic company culture, and legal battles over intellectual property theft. These issues culminated in a viral blog post by former engineer Susan Fowler, detailing systemic sexism and harassment at Uber. This post sparked an internal investigation and led to significant public backlash.

## Stepping Down, Moving Forward

The mounting controversies and pressure from investors eventually led to Kalanick's resignation as CEO in June 2017. His departure marked a dramatic turning point for Uber. Despite stepping down, Kalanick remained on Uber's board and retained a significant stake in the company. His exit allowed Uber to begin the process of rebuilding its reputation and addressing the systemic issues that had come to light.

In 2019, Uber went public, achieving a valuation of $82 billion. This milestone underscored the transformative impact of Kalanick's vision, despite the controversies and challenges that had marred his tenure. Kalanick's role in building Uber into a global transportation giant remains a significant part of his legacy.

## Lessons from the Edge of Innovation

Travis Kalanick's journey offers profound insights into the power of disruptive innovation, resilience, and the complexities of leadership. "Disruption means taking risks and challenging the status quo," Kalanick has often said. His ability to envision and execute a radically new approach to urban transportation was instrumental in Uber's success.

Kalanick also highlights the importance of resilience and adaptability. "Building a transformative company requires navigating through storms and learning from setbacks," he advises aspiring entrepreneurs. His journey reflects the dual-edged nature of disruptive innovation, where bold strategies can lead to both remarkable success and significant controversy.

## Leaving a Complex Legacy

Looking ahead, Kalanick remains involved in the tech industry through his investment fund, 10100, and his new venture, CloudKitchens, which focuses on ghost kitchens for food delivery services. His influence on the transportation and tech industries is undeniable, and his ventures continue to push the boundaries of innovation.

Kalanick's legacy at Uber is complex, marked by both transformative impact and significant controversy. His contributions to the rise of the gig economy and the reshaping of urban mobility are monumental, setting new standards and challenges for future innovators. His journey serves as a compelling reminder of the power and pitfalls of disruptive innovation.

## Conclusion

Travis Kalanick's journey from a young tech enthusiast to the co-founder of Uber showcases the power of disruptive innovation, unyielding resilience, and visionary leadership. Despite facing numerous challenges, including legal battles, market skepticism, and internal controversies, Kalanick's relentless drive transformed Uber from a bold idea into a global transportation behemoth.

# Marc Barros

## Capturing Adventure with Contour

Born in Seattle, Washington, in 1980, Marc Barros grew up with a love for the outdoors and technology. His father, an engineer, and his mother, a schoolteacher, provided a supportive environment that nurtured his curiosity and ambition. Barros attended the University of Washington, where he studied business administration. It was here that he would embark on a path that would lead him to co-found Contour.

## Dreams to High-Altitude Realities

Barros' entrepreneurial journey began with a senior project at the University of Washington. Inspired by his passion for skiing and the desire to capture his adventures, Barros teamed up with Jason Green to create a hands-free video camera. The initial prototype, built in their dorm room, was a rudimentary helmet-mounted camera that used a tape recorder to capture footage. Despite its simplicity, the idea had potential, and Barros was determined to turn it into a viable business.

## The Dorm Room Project That Took Off

In 2004, Barros and Green founded VholdR, which would later be rebranded as Contour. With minimal resources and no external funding, they bootstrapped the company, focusing on developing a wearable camera that could capture high-quality video in extreme conditions. Barros took on multiple roles, from designing the product to handling marketing and sales. The early days were filled with challenges, including technical difficulties and financial constraints. However, Barros' determination and innovative spirit kept the project alive.

One of the most dramatic moments in Contour's early journey came when they secured a meeting with REI, a major outdoor retailer. Barros personally demonstrated the camera's capabilities, capturing his own skiing footage. Impressed by the product's potential, REI placed a significant order, providing the validation and funding needed to continue development.

## Turning an Idea into an Action Camera Pioneer

Building Contour was fraught with adversity. The action camera market was nascent, and Barros faced intense competition from better-funded rivals, particularly GoPro. Securing funding was a constant struggle, and Barros often had to make tough decisions to keep the company afloat. One particularly challenging period came when Contour ran out of money just as they were preparing to launch a new product. In a bold move, Barros decided to take out a personal loan to cover production costs, demonstrating his unwavering commitment to the company's success.

Despite these challenges, Contour began to gain traction. The company introduced the ContourHD in 2009, the world's first HD wearable camera, which received widespread acclaim for its quality and ease of use. This innovation helped Contour carve out a niche in the action camera market and build a loyal customer base.

## Capturing Adventure

By 2011, Contour had established itself as a significant player in the action camera industry, competing head-to-head with GoPro. The company's products were sold in major retail stores, and they had secured partnerships with leading outdoor brands. Barros' focus on innovation and customer experience was paying off, driving growth and expanding Contour's market reach.

One of the most intense and transformative periods in Contour's history came in 2012, when the company was named to Inc. Magazine's list of the fastest-growing private companies in America. This recognition validated Barros' vision and hard work, and it seemed that Contour was on the path to long-term success.

## Facing the Avalanche

However, the journey was not without setbacks. In 2013, Contour faced significant financial challenges, struggling to compete with GoPro's aggressive marketing and rapid product development. The company's growth stalled, and internal conflicts began to surface. Despite Barros' best efforts to steer the company through turbulent waters, Contour eventually ran out of capital. In a dramatic and unexpected turn of events, Contour was forced to shut down operations in 2013, laying off its entire staff.

This period was particularly challenging for Barros, who had poured his heart and soul into building Contour. The closure was a significant blow, both professionally and personally. However, Barros' resilience and entrepreneurial spirit remained intact.

## Pivot and Rebirth

In 2014, less than a year after its closure, Contour was revived under new ownership. Barros, although no longer involved with the day-to-day operations, remained a passionate advocate for the brand and continued to innovate in the tech space. He shifted his focus to new ventures, drawing on his experiences with Contour to mentor other entrepreneurs and develop new products.

Barros' ability to pivot and find new opportunities after such a dramatic setback underscores his resilience and determination. His journey with Contour provided valuable lessons in leadership, innovation, and the importance of perseverance.

## Insights from the Summit

Marc Barros' journey offers profound insights into the power of innovation, resilience, and adaptability. "Success is about creating products that solve real problems and staying committed to your vision, even when faced with adversity," Barros often emphasizes. His ability to navigate challenges and maintain a clear focus on product quality and customer experience was key to Contour's initial success.

Barros also highlights the importance of learning from failures. "Every setback is an opportunity to learn and grow," he advises aspiring entrepreneurs. His journey reflects the impact of resilience and the ability to pivot and adapt in response to changing market conditions.

## Marc Barros' Continuing Impact

Looking ahead, Barros continues to be involved in the tech and startup communities. He has launched Moment, a company specializing in photography gear for smartphones, where he applies the lessons learned from his time at Contour to build innovative products. His influence extends beyond his ventures, as he actively mentors young entrepreneurs and shares his insights on building successful businesses.

Barros' legacy at Contour is one of innovation and perseverance. His contributions to the action camera market helped shape the industry and set new standards for wearable technology. His journey serves as an inspiring reminder of the power of resilience and the importance of staying true to one's vision.

## Conclusion

Marc Barros' story is a powerful illustration of resilience, innovation, and commitment to quality. From his humble beginnings as a student passionate about skiing to founding Contour, a pioneering company in the action camera industry, Barros has shown unwavering determination in the face of challenges. His journey is marked by bold decisions and a relentless drive to enhance user experience.

Despite financial setbacks and fierce competition, Barros has proven that every failure is an opportunity to learn and reinvent oneself. His ongoing involvement in the tech sector, through initiatives like Moment and mentoring young entrepreneurs, showcases his indomitable entrepreneurial spirit.

# Lisa Price

## From Kitchen Alchemist to Beauty Mogul

Born on May 18, 1962, in Brooklyn, New York, Lisa Price grew up in a creative and nurturing environment. Her mother, Carol, was a strong and supportive figure who encouraged Price's artistic inclinations. Despite facing financial hardships, Price's family instilled in her the values of hard work and determination, which would later become the foundation of her entrepreneurial journey.

## Turning Kitchen Concoctions into a Beauty Empire

Price's entrepreneurial journey began in the early 1990s, not as a strategic business plan but as a personal passion. Working in television production, Price spent her spare time experimenting with homemade beauty products in her kitchen. Inspired by her love for fragrance and natural ingredients, she started crafting lotions, creams, and hair care products using essential oils and natural extracts. What began as a hobby quickly garnered attention from friends and family, who were captivated by the quality and effectiveness of her creations.

In 1993, encouraged by her mother, Price sold her products at a local church flea market. The response was overwhelmingly positive, and Price realized that her homemade concoctions had the potential to become a successful business. She named her company Carol's Daughter in honor of her mother, whose support and encouragement had been instrumental in her journey.

## Risking It All

With no formal training in business or cosmetology, Price faced significant challenges in turning her kitchen-based hobby into a viable enterprise. She started by selling her products at local flea markets and craft fairs, gradually building a loyal customer base. Price's emphasis on quality, natural ingredients, and addressing the specific needs of Black women set Carol's Daughter apart from other beauty brands.

One of the most dramatic moments in the early days came when Price decided to invest her life savings into opening a small store in Brooklyn in 1999. This bold move was fraught with risk, as she had no guarantee of success. Despite her fears, Price's store quickly became a community hub, attracting a diverse clientele who appreciated her commitment to natural beauty products.

## A Star-Studded Rise to Fame

Carol's Daughter began to gain national recognition in the mid-2000s, thanks in part to high-profile endorsements from celebrities like Jada Pinkett Smith, Mary J. Blige, and Oprah Winfrey. However, it was her appearance on The Oprah Winfrey Show that proved to be a game-changer. In an interview, Price shares how this opportunity arose through a connection made at a party, highlighting the power of networking. The appearance on Oprah provided significant validation for her brand and led to a surge in popularity and sales.

This moment underscored the importance of manifesting dreams and seizing opportunities, empowering Price and her business in unprecedented ways.

## Overcoming Financial Storms with Unwavering Faith

Building Carol's Daughter was not without its challenges. Price faced significant financial struggles, often relying on credit cards and personal loans to keep the business afloat. Additionally, she encountered skepticism from mainstream retailers who doubted the market potential for a niche beauty brand targeting BIPOC women.

One particularly challenging period came in the early 2000s when Price's business experienced a severe cash flow crisis. Determined to keep Carol's Daughter alive, she reached out to friends and family for support and took on multiple side jobs to cover expenses. This period tested her resilience and commitment, but Price's unwavering belief in her vision helped her navigate through the crisis.

## Triumph and Transformation

Carol's Daughter began to gain national recognition in the mid-2000s, thanks in part to high-profile endorsements from celebrities like Jada Pinkett Smith, Mary J. Blige, and Oprah Winfrey. These endorsements helped propel the brand into the mainstream, attracting a broader customer base and increasing sales.

One of the most transformative moments in Carol's Daughter's history came in 2014 when the company was acquired by L'Oréal. This acquisition provided the resources and infrastructure needed to scale the business globally while maintaining its commitment to natural ingredients and addressing the unique needs of women of color. The partnership with L'Oréal validated Price's vision and hard work, marking a significant milestone in her entrepreneurial journey.

## Insights from a Beauty Mogul

Lisa Price's journey offers valuable insights into the power of passion, resilience, and staying true to one's values. "Success is about more than just making money; it's about creating something that has meaning and impact," Price often emphasizes. Her ability to turn a personal passion into a transformative business highlights the importance of authenticity and dedication.

Price also stresses the importance of perseverance and community. "Building a business requires a strong support system and a willingness to overcome obstacles," she advises aspiring entrepreneurs. Her journey reflects the power of community and the impact of creating products that resonate with a diverse and underserved market.

## Beyond Beauty

Looking ahead, Price remains committed to her mission of empowering women and promoting natural beauty. She continues to innovate within the Carol's Daughter brand, exploring new product lines and expanding the company's reach. Her focus includes leveraging digital platforms to connect with a global audience and provide educational resources on natural beauty and self-care.

Price's influence extends beyond Carol's Daughter. She actively supports initiatives that promote entrepreneurship and diversity in the beauty industry, reflecting her belief in the power of inclusive representation. Her work has inspired a new generation of entrepreneurs to pursue their passions and create impactful solutions.

## Conclusion

Lisa Price's story is a powerful example of how passion, resilience, and a commitment to authenticity can lead to extraordinary success. From her early challenges in launching Carol's Daughter to building a transformative beauty brand that has redefined natural beauty for women of color, Price's journey is marked by bold decisions and an unwavering dedication to her vision. Her ability to navigate intense challenges and turn opportunities into transformative success has set a new standard in the beauty industry. Price's journey serves as an inspiring reminder that with determination and a clear mission, any obstacle can be overcome.

# David Heath

## Revolutionizing Comfort and Giving with Bombas

Born in New York City in 1984, David Heath grew up in a family that valued hard work and community service. His parents, both involved in local charities, instilled in him the importance of helping others from a young age. This ethos would later become a cornerstone of his entrepreneurial journey.

### Turning Compassion into Action

Heath's entrepreneurial spark ignited in 2011 when he came across a Facebook post stating that socks were the most requested item at homeless shelters. This simple yet profound piece of information struck a chord with him. Realizing that such a basic necessity was in high demand, Heath saw an opportunity to create a business that could make a meaningful difference.

Determined to turn this insight into action, Heath quit his stable job and teamed up with his friend Randy Goldberg. Together, they envisioned a company that would not only produce high-quality socks but also give back to those in need. The idea was simple yet powerful: for every pair of socks sold, a pair would be donated to a homeless shelter. This one-for-one business model would become the foundation of Bombas.

## Sock it to Poverty

In 2013, Heath and Goldberg launched Bombas, named after the Latin word for bumblebee, symbolizing the small yet impactful contribution they aimed to make. The journey was fraught with challenges that went beyond the typical funding and scaling issues. Heath and his team faced the daunting task of creating a product that could stand out in a crowded market while staying true to their mission-driven ethos.

One of the most dramatic challenges came early on when Heath discovered that traditional socks were not designed to meet the needs of homeless individuals. Many homeless people suffer from foot problems due to inadequate footwear. Determined to address this, Heath spent countless hours researching and redesigning socks to include features like reinforced seams, antimicrobial treatment, and extra cushioning. This commitment to quality and functionality became a hallmark of Bombas socks.

## Threading Through Challenges

Building Bombas was not just about creating a great product; it was about embedding a culture of giving and empathy into the company's DNA. Heath faced significant personal and emotional challenges as he sought to maintain this balance. One particularly intense moment came during a visit to a homeless shelter, where he saw firsthand the dire conditions and the impact of their donations. This experience reaffirmed his commitment but also highlighted the enormous responsibility he felt towards the mission.

Additionally, Heath had to combat the stigma and skepticism

surrounding for-profit companies that engage in philanthropy. Critics questioned the sincerity and sustainability of Bombas' model. To prove them wrong, Heath focused on transparency and authenticity, ensuring that the company's mission was not just a marketing gimmick but a genuine commitment to social good.

## Walking the Walk

Bombas' growth was both rapid and impactful. By 2016, the company had donated over a million pairs of socks, a milestone that validated Heath's vision and hard work. The company's emphasis on quality and social impact resonated with consumers, driving significant sales and customer loyalty.

One of the most dramatic periods in Bombas' history came in 2018 when Heath and his team faced a severe supply chain disruption that threatened to delay deliveries and donations. In a bold move, Heath personally negotiated with suppliers and logistics partners, working around the clock to ensure that Bombas met its commitments. This crisis tested his leadership and resilience but ultimately strengthened the company's operations and resolve.

## Rapid Growth and Unwavering Commitment

David Heath's journey offers profound insights into the power of mission-driven entrepreneurship, resilience, and the importance of empathy. "Success is about more than profit; it's about making a meaningful difference in the world," Heath often emphasizes. His ability to create a product that not only met a market need but also addressed a critical social issue was key to Bombas' success.

Heath also stresses the importance of authenticity and staying true to one's values. "Building a mission-driven company requires unwavering commitment and transparency," he advises aspiring entrepreneurs. His journey reflects the power of aligning business goals with social impact, demonstrating that profitability and philanthropy can go hand in hand.

## Expanding Impact with Every Pair

Looking ahead, Heath remains committed to expanding Bombas' impact. He envisions further growth and innovation, including developing new products and expanding the company's giving model to address other essential needs. His focus includes leveraging technology and partnerships to enhance the company's efficiency and reach.

Heath's influence extends beyond Bombas. He actively supports initiatives that promote social entrepreneurship and corporate responsibility, reflecting his belief in the power of business to drive positive change. His work has inspired a new generation of entrepreneurs to pursue mission-driven ventures and create lasting impact.

## Conclusion

David Heath's story is a powerful example of how compassion, resilience, and a commitment to social impact can lead to extraordinary success. From his early challenges in launching Bombas to building a transformative company that redefined socks and corporate giving, Heath's journey is marked by bold decisions and an unwavering dedication to his vision. His ability to navigate intense challenges and turn opportunities into transformative success has set a new standard in social entrepreneurship.

# James Park

## From Harvard Dropout to Fitness Tech Titan

James Park was born in Seoul, South Korea, in 1976 and moved to the United States at a young age. Growing up in northern California, he developed a passion for technology and entrepreneurship early on. Inspired by his parents, who ran various small businesses, Park attended Harvard University to study computer science but dropped out to pursue his entrepreneurial ambitions.

## A Personal Frustration Sparks an Idea

Park's entrepreneurial journey included several tech startups, but a personal frustration led to the idea for Fitbit. In 2007, while brainstorming with his friend and future co-founder Eric Friedman, Park was inspired by the Nintendo Wii. He realized the potential of leveraging sensors and wireless technology to help people lead healthier lives, sparking the idea for a wearable device that could track fitness and health metrics.

## Building the Dream

In 2007, Park and Friedman founded Fitbit with the goal of revolutionizing fitness tracking. Their journey was fraught with challenges, including technical difficulties and investor skepticism. One dramatic moment came when they ran out of funds just before launching their first product. Determined to succeed, they maxed out their credit cards to cover manufacturing costs, demonstrating their unwavering commitment to Fitbit's success.

## Turning Challenges into Triumphs

Creating Fitbit was not just about developing a great product but also overcoming numerous obstacles. Ensuring the accuracy and reliability of the fitness tracker was a significant challenge, as early prototypes faced technical issues. Park's resilience shone as he worked tirelessly with his team to refine the product.

Competition from larger tech companies was another major hurdle. To differentiate Fitbit, Park focused on creating a strong brand identity and community around health and fitness. This strategy paid off, quickly gaining Fitbit a loyal user base and widespread recognition.

## Rapid Growth and IPO Success

Fitbit's growth was rapid and transformative. By 2013, the company had sold millions of devices and established itself as a leader in the fitness tracking industry. Park's emphasis on user experience and continuous innovation kept Fitbit ahead of the competition.

The company's IPO in 2015 was a significant milestone, valuing Fitbit at over $4 billion. This success validated Park's vision and hard work, highlighting Fitbit's impact on the fitness and health industry.

## Vision and Resilience

James Park's journey offers profound insights into the importance of innovation, resilience, and user-centric design. "Success comes from creating products that people love and that make a real difference in their lives," Park often emphasizes. His ability to turn a personal frustration into a groundbreaking product highlights the power of understanding and addressing user needs. Park also stresses the importance of perseverance and adaptability. "Building a business requires navigating challenges and staying focused on your mission," he advises aspiring entrepreneurs. His journey reflects the power of determination and the impact of staying true to one's vision.

## Navigating Competition and Industry Changes

By 2013, Fitbit faced increasing competition from tech giants like Nike and Jawbone. Despite this, Fitbit maintained its market lead through continuous innovation and a strong community-driven approach. Park remained cautious, acknowledging the challenges but focusing on the company's strengths.

## The Impact of the Apple Watch

The release of the Apple Watch in 2015 posed a significant challenge. Despite initial concerns, Park believed in Fitbit's simpler, user-focused product. However, the competition eventually led to a 75% drop in Fitbit's stock by 2016, highlighting the need for strategic pivots.

## Pivoting Towards Health Data and Analytics

By 2019, Fitbit shifted its focus from hardware to healthcare data and behavior change, integrating advanced health metrics and personalized insights. This pivot was crucial for adapting to industry changes and maintaining relevance.

## The Google Acquisition: A Strategic Move

In 2019, Google announced its intent to acquire Fitbit for $2.1 billion. For Park, this move was about ensuring Fitbit's legacy and leveraging Google's resources to enhance their mission. The acquisition aimed to drive innovation in remote healthcare and behavior change, reflecting the evolving landscape of health technology.

## Conclusion

James Park's story is a testament to vision, resilience, and the power of innovation. From overcoming early financial struggles and technical challenges to leading Fitbit through an era of unprecedented growth, Park's journey underscores the importance of perseverance in building a transformative product. His dedication to enhancing health and wellness through technology has left a lasting impact, inspiring future entrepreneurs to tackle big challenges and create products that truly make a difference in people's lives. Park's legacy is one of relentless pursuit of excellence, showing that with passion and commitment, one can turn an idea into a global success.

# Alexa Von Tobel

## From Ivy League to Fintech Queen

Born in Jacksonville, Florida, in 1984, Alexa Von Tobel grew up in a supportive family that valued education and hard work. Her parents, both entrepreneurs, inspired her to pursue her own path in the business world. Von Tobel attended Harvard University, where she studied psychology before pursuing an MBA at Harvard Business School. However, her passion for financial literacy would soon lead her to take a bold leap.

## The "Aha" Moment

Von Tobel's entrepreneurial journey began with a personal frustration: despite her Ivy League education, she realized she lacked practical knowledge about managing personal finances. This gap in financial literacy became glaringly apparent during her time at Harvard Business School. She observed that many of her peers also struggled with financial planning, budgeting, and investing. Recognizing a significant market need, Von Tobel envisioned a platform that would provide accessible and comprehensive financial planning for individuals and families.

In 2008, amidst the financial crisis, Von Tobel took a leave of absence from Harvard Business School to pursue her vision. She poured her savings into developing the concept for LearnVest, a platform designed to offer affordable, high-quality financial advice and tools to help users manage their money more effectively.

## Building from a Tiny NYC Apartment

With no prior experience in financial services, Von Tobel faced significant challenges in getting LearnVest off the ground. She moved to New York City and began building her company from her small apartment, working tirelessly to develop the platform and secure initial funding. Her determination paid off when she secured seed funding from prominent investors, including Accel Partners and Marc Andreessen.

One of the most dramatic moments in LearnVest's early days came when Von Tobel pitched her idea to a room full of seasoned venture capitalists. She was the only woman in the room and had to overcome significant skepticism. Despite the pressure, Von Tobel's passion and clear vision for LearnVest impressed the investors, securing the funding needed to launch the platform.

## Conquering the Finance World One Pitch at a Time

Building LearnVest was fraught with adversity. The financial services industry is heavily regulated and dominated by established players, making it difficult for a new entrant to gain traction. Von Tobel faced numerous challenges, from navigating complex regulatory requirements to building a robust technology platform that could handle the needs of her users.

In a particularly challenging period, Von Tobel struggled to balance the demands of raising capital, managing a growing team, and continuously improving the product. Despite these pressures, she remained focused on her mission to democratize financial planning. Her relentless drive and innovative approach helped LearnVest differentiate itself in a crowded market.

## Turning Setbacks into Comebacks

LearnVest's growth was rapid and transformative. By 2012, the platform had attracted over 100,000 users and had expanded its offerings to include personalized financial plans, budgeting tools, and educational resources. Von Tobel's focus on user experience and accessibility resonated with a wide audience, driving significant user engagement and growth.

One of the most intense and transformative periods in LearnVest's history came in 2015, when the company was acquired by Northwestern Mutual for a reported $375 million. This acquisition marked a significant milestone for Von Tobel and validated her vision of making financial planning accessible to all. The partnership with Northwestern Mutual provided the resources and infrastructure needed to scale LearnVest's impact and reach even more users.

## The LearnVest Milestone

Alexa Von Tobel's journey offers valuable insights into the power of resilience, innovation, and a commitment to solving real-world problems. "Success comes from identifying a genuine need and creating a solution that makes a meaningful impact," Von Tobel often emphasizes. Her ability to turn a personal frustration into a transformative business highlights the importance of understanding and addressing market needs.

Von Tobel also stresses the importance of perseverance and adaptability. "Building a business requires navigating challenges and staying focused on your mission, even when faced with setbacks," she advises aspiring entrepreneurs. Her journey reflects the power of determination and the impact of staying true to one's vision.

## The Future of Financial Empowerment

Looking ahead, Von Tobel remains committed to empowering individuals with the tools and knowledge to achieve financial wellness. She continues to be a prominent advocate for financial literacy and education, sharing her insights through speaking engagements, her book "Financially Fearless," and her podcast "The Founders Project."

Von Tobel's influence extends beyond LearnVest. She actively supports initiatives that promote entrepreneurship and financial literacy, reflecting her belief in the power of knowledge and innovation to drive positive change. Her work has inspired a new generation of entrepreneurs to pursue their visions and create impactful solutions.

## Conclusion

Alexa Von Tobel's story is a powerful example of how resilience, innovation, and a commitment to solving real-world problems can lead to extraordinary success. From her early challenges in launching LearnVest to building a transformative financial platform, Von Tobel's journey is marked by bold decisions and an unwavering dedication to her vision. Her ability to navigate intense challenges and turn opportunities into transformative success has set a new standard in the financial services industry.

ALEXA VON TOBEL

# Tom Preston-Werner

## From Code Dreamer to GitHub Guru

Born in 1979 in Dubuque, Iowa, Tom Preston-Werner grew up in a household that celebrated curiosity and learning. With a computer science professor for a father and a librarian for a mother, Tom was surrounded by an environment that valued intellectual exploration. This nurturing atmosphere set the stage for his lifelong fascination with technology and open-source software.

## From College to Code

After earning his degree in physics from Harvey Mudd College, Tom moved to San Francisco to immerse himself in the tech startup scene. It was during his tenure at various startups that he recognized the inefficiencies of existing version control systems. The lack of collaborative features sparked an idea in Tom's mind, leading him to envision a platform that would revolutionize how developers worked together on code.

## The Power Trio

In 2007, while working at Powerset, Tom met Chris Wanstrath and PJ Hyett. The trio shared a vision of transforming software collaboration, leading to the birth of GitHub in 2008. Their goal was clear: to create a user-friendly platform that would make version control and code collaboration seamless and intuitive. The journey was fraught with challenges, but their belief in the power of open-source collaboration kept them moving forward.

## Taking the Leap

One of the most pivotal moments in Tom's career was his decision to leave his secure job at Powerset to devote himself entirely to GitHub. This risky move underscored his commitment to the project and his vision for what GitHub could become. His dedication paid off as the platform quickly gained popularity among developers.

## Scaling New Heights

The rapid growth of GitHub brought its own set of challenges. Ensuring scalability and reliability was a constant struggle as the user base expanded. Tom and his team worked tirelessly to maintain the platform's performance, often pulling all-nighters to solve critical issues. Additionally, competition from established version control systems pushed them to continually innovate and improve GitHub's features.

## Born to Innovate

GitHub's breakthrough came in 2012 when the platform secured a $100 million investment from Andreessen Horowitz. This investment validated Tom's vision and provided the resources needed to scale the platform globally. The most dramatic milestone, however, was in 2018 when Microsoft acquired GitHub for $7.5 billion, marking a significant achievement in Tom's entrepreneurial journey.

## The Tools of a Visionary: Tom's Tech Arsenal

Tom's unique approach to work extended beyond his visionary ideas. In interviews, he humorously shared his preference for tater tots and beer, along with insights into his tech setup. His primary machine was a high-powered MacBook Pro, and he frequently used tools like TextMate, Terminal.app, and Google Chrome. Tom's dream setup? An elaborate, futuristic coding environment with a wrap-around display and a powerful sound system, illustrating his blend of practicality and imagination.

## Lessons from the Journey

Tom's journey offers rich insights into innovation, resilience, and the power of community. He often emphasizes the importance of creating tools that empower and foster collaboration. His experience highlights the necessity of perseverance and adaptability in the face of challenges. For Tom, innovation stems from dissatisfaction with the status quo, driving him to push boundaries and share ideas with the world.

## Beyond GitHub

After leaving GitHub, Tom continued to explore new frontiers in technology. He co-founded Chatterbug, a language learning platform, and remained active in various tech ventures and open-source projects. His dedication to fostering innovation and supporting the tech community persisted, as did his advocacy for diversity and inclusion in the industry.

## Conclusion

Tom Preston-Werner's story is a testament to the transformative power of innovation and community. From the early challenges of launching GitHub to its monumental success, Tom's journey is characterized by bold decisions and an unwavering commitment to his vision. His ability to navigate obstacles and seize opportunities has set a new standard in the tech industry. Tom's legacy extends beyond GitHub, inspiring a new generation of developers to dream big and collaborate openly. His journey reminds us that with passion, resilience, and a clear mission, even the most ambitious goals are within reach.

# Alekseï Pajitnov

## From Soviet Labs to Global Obsession

Born on March 14, 1956, in Moscow, Alekseï Pajitnov grew up in a culturally rich environment, with a mother who was a journalist and a father who was an art critic. This background instilled in him a deep appreciation for art and creativity. Pajitnov's passion for puzzles and games was evident from a young age, setting the stage for his future contributions to the world of gaming.

## The Evolving Mind

Pajitnov's academic journey led him to the Moscow Institute of Aviation, where he studied applied mathematics. His education fostered a deep understanding of complex systems, which would later play a critical role in his game design. In the early 1980s, Pajitnov began working at the Dorodnitsyn Computing Centre of the Soviet Academy of Sciences. It was here, amidst the computing machinery of the time, that Pajitnov started exploring the idea of creating digital puzzles on the Elektronika 60, a Soviet computer. Inspired by his favorite puzzle game, pentominoes, he envisioned a game that would challenge players to fit falling shapes into a grid.

## The Birth of an Iconic Game

In 1984, Pajitnov developed the prototype for what would become Tetris. The game's simplicity and addictive nature quickly captivated those who played it. Despite being developed in a Soviet research lab, Tetris transcended its origins and began to spread beyond the Iron Curtain. The minimalist design, with no flashy graphics or sound, emphasized the game's core mechanics and addictive gameplay.

## The Journey to Global Fame

Pajitnov's journey to bring Tetris to the world was fraught with challenges, many of which stemmed from the political and economic environment of the Soviet Union. Unlike Western countries, where game developers could easily commercialize their creations, Soviet scientists did not own the rights to their work. This meant Pajitnov had to navigate a complex web of bureaucratic hurdles to share Tetris with a wider audience.

## The Battle for Tetris

The journey to commercialize Tetris was marked by intense legal battles and complex negotiations. The Soviet Union's bureaucratic machinery was ill-equipped to handle intellectual property rights, and multiple parties claimed ownership and distribution rights to Tetris. One particularly intense period came in the late 1980s when multiple companies, including Nintendo and Atari, vied for the rights to distribute Tetris on home consoles. The legal disputes culminated in a dramatic showdown, with Nintendo ultimately securing the rights to Tetris for its Game Boy console. This move proved to be a game-changer, as Tetris became a global phenomenon, selling millions of copies and cementing its place in gaming history.

## A Leap of Faith

In 1991, amid the changing political landscape of the Soviet Union, Pajitnov moved to the United States. This move marked a new chapter in his career, allowing him to fully engage with the burgeoning video game industry. Pajitnov joined Microsoft in 1996, where he continued to develop puzzle games and contribute to the field he had helped pioneer.

## Co-Founding The Tetris Company

Despite Tetris's monumental success, Pajitnov initially saw little financial benefit from his creation due to the complexities of Soviet intellectual property laws. It wasn't until 1996, after the dissolution of the Soviet Union, that Pajitnov co-founded The Tetris Company with Henk Rogers, a businessman who had been instrumental in securing the rights for Nintendo. This partnership allowed Pajitnov to finally receive royalties from his creation and take control of Tetris's future.

## The Modern Puzzle Master

Even after the monumental success of Tetris, Pajitnov's passion for game design remained undiminished. He continued to create new puzzles and games, constantly pushing the boundaries of the genre. His later works include titles like Hexic and Pandora's Box, which further cemented his reputation as a master of puzzle design.

## The Tools of Creativity

Pajitnov's approach to game development is rooted in his fascination with mathematical puzzles and logical challenges. He often emphasizes the importance of simplicity and elegance in game design, a philosophy that is clearly reflected in the enduring appeal of Tetris. Pajitnov's ability to create engaging and accessible games has inspired countless developers and shaped the landscape of modern gaming.

## The power of resilience

Alekseï Pajitnov's journey offers valuable insights into the power of creativity, resilience, and adaptability. "Tetris is a game that transcends cultural and linguistic barriers," Pajitnov often emphasizes. His ability to create a universally appealing game from a simple concept highlights the importance of innovation and staying true to one's passions. Pajitnov also stresses the importance of perseverance in the face of adversity. "Bringing Tetris to the world required navigating complex challenges and maintaining a long-term vision," he advises aspiring creators.

## A Legacy of Blocks

Alekseï Pajitnov's legacy extends far beyond the creation of a single game. Tetris has become a cultural phenomenon, influencing everything from game design to neuroscience research. Pajitnov's innovative spirit and dedication to his craft continue to inspire new generations of game developers and puzzle enthusiasts around the world. His work has inspired a new generation of game developers to pursue their visions and create experiences that resonate with people worldwide.

## Conclusion

Alekseï Pajitnov's story is a testament to the transformative power of creativity and perseverance. From his early days in the Soviet Union to his contributions to the global gaming industry, Pajitnov has left an indelible mark on the world. His journey from a young puzzle enthusiast to the creator of one of the most iconic video games of all time exemplifies the impact of visionary thinking and relentless pursuit of passion. Pajitnov's legacy continues to shape the future of game design, reminding us that with imagination and dedication, the simplest ideas can lead to the most extraordinary outcomes.

# Jessica Herrin

## Empowering Women Through Innovation

Born in 1972, Jessica Herrin's upbringing in Austin, Texas, laid the foundation for her entrepreneurial spirit. Her parents, who valued hard work and determination, nurtured her ambitions and fostered a drive for success from an early age. Herrin's early life was marked by a natural inclination towards leadership and creativity.

## The Birth of a Serial Entrepreneur

Herrin's entrepreneurial journey began at Stanford University, where she immersed herself in the dynamic world of Silicon Valley startups. In 1996, she co-founded Della & James, an online bridal registry that eventually merged with WeddingChannel.com. This venture provided her with invaluable experience in building and scaling a startup, setting the stage for her future endeavors.

## A Vision Realized

In 2003, after taking time to focus on her growing family, Herrin was inspired by her passion for jewelry and her desire to empower women. This led to the creation of Luxe Jewels, which rebranded as Stella & Dot in 2007. Named after her grandmothers, the company symbolized strength, style, and the empowerment of women. Herrin's vision was to create flexible career opportunities for women through a modern direct sales model that combined e-commerce with personal touch.

## Navigating Challenges and Achieving Success

Building Stella & Dot was fraught with challenges, including skepticism from investors and the economic downturn during the 2008 financial crisis. However, Herrin's innovative approach and unwavering commitment to her vision allowed the company to thrive. By focusing on empowering her network of stylists and providing them with the tools to succeed, Stella & Dot weathered the storm and emerged stronger.

In 2011, the company received a significant investment from Sequoia Capital, validating Herrin's vision and providing the resources needed to scale the business internationally. Stella & Dot expanded its product lines to include accessories, bags, and clothing, and launched sister brands Keep Collective and EVER Skincare, further diversifying its offerings.

## The Power of Empowerment

Jessica Herrin's journey highlights the importance of innovation, resilience, and empowerment. She often emphasizes that success is about creating opportunities for others and making a positive impact.

Her ability to combine the direct sales model with modern technology underscores the importance of adaptability in achieving business success.

Herrin also stresses the value of perseverance and staying true to one's mission, advising aspiring entrepreneurs to navigate challenges with determination and a clear vision.

## A Legacy of Empowerment and Innovation

Looking ahead, Herrin remains committed to advancing Stella & Dot's mission of empowering women through entrepreneurship. She envisions further growth and innovation, including expanding the company's product offerings and enhancing the digital platform to provide even more support for stylists.

Beyond Stella & Dot, Herrin actively supports initiatives that promote female entrepreneurship and leadership. Her influence has inspired a new generation of female entrepreneurs to pursue their dreams and create impactful businesses.

## Conclusion

Jessica Herrin's story is a testament to the transformative power of innovation, resilience, and a commitment to empowering others. From her early days co-founding Della & James to building Stella & Dot into a global brand, Herrin's journey is marked by bold decisions and an unwavering dedication to her vision. Her ability to navigate challenges and turn opportunities into success has set a new standard in the direct sales and e-commerce industries.

# Chris Barton

## The Early Inventor

Born on October 2, 1972, in Chicago, Illinois, Chris Barton displayed a keen curiosity and innovative spirit from a young age. He pursued his undergraduate studies at the University of California, Berkeley, earning a degree in Business Administration. His academic journey continued at the University of Cambridge, where he completed an M.Phil in Economics, followed by an MBA from Stanford University. These educational experiences equipped Barton with a solid foundation in both technology and business, setting the stage for his future entrepreneurial ventures.

## The Musical Eureka Moment

The idea for Shazam was born out of a common frustration: not being able to identify a song playing on the radio or in a public place. In 1999, Barton co-founded Shazam with three friends, Dhiraj Mukherjee, Philip Inghelbrecht, and Avery Wang. Their mission was to create a technology that could identify music through sound alone. The challenge was immense, as it required developing a sophisticated algorithm capable of recognizing songs from a vast database, even in noisy environments. Barton often says, "Innovation often stems from exploring what else can be done with existing resources or technologies."

## A Technological Feat

The early days of Shazam were marked by intensive research and development. Avery Wang, the technical co-founder, played a crucial role in developing the core audio recognition technology. This involved creating a unique fingerprint for each song, which the Shazam app could then match against a vast database. The technology had to be incredibly precise, given the complexities of ambient noise and varying audio quality.

One of the most significant milestones in Shazam's history was its launch in 2002. Initially, users would dial a shortcode on their phones, hold the phone up to the music source, and receive an SMS with the song details. This early version of Shazam laid the groundwork for what would become a revolutionary app.

## Crafting the Magic

Building Shazam was not without its challenges. The company faced technical hurdles in perfecting the music recognition algorithm and significant financial pressures. In the early 2000s, the concept of a music recognition service was novel, and securing funding was difficult. However, Barton's perseverance and strategic thinking helped Shazam navigate these obstacles. "Persistence and continuous innovation are essential; never assume past success guarantees future relevance," Barton often advises.

Reflecting on this period, Barton said, "From 2002 to the launch of the App Store on iPhones in 2008, we came nowhere close to having enough users. So we were burning cash, we were near bankruptcy, we had multiple rounds of layoffs, and we were barely surviving as a company."

A critical turning point came with the advent of the smartphone era. The launch of the iPhone in 2007 provided the perfect platform for Shazam to thrive. The app's integration with iOS allowed users to identify songs with a single tap, significantly enhancing the user experience. This adaptation to new technology was crucial in ensuring Shazam's continued relevance and growth.

## Tech Triumphs and Trials

Shazam's growth was rapid and transformative. By 2018, the app had been downloaded over 1 billion times and boasted more than 150 million active users each month. One of the most dramatic periods in Shazam's history came when Apple acquired the company in 2018 for an estimated $400 million. This acquisition validated Barton's vision and marked a significant achievement in his entrepreneurial journey.

## Wisdom from a Tech Pioneer

Chris Barton's journey offers valuable insights into the power of innovation, resilience, and strategic adaptation. "Innovation is about seeing what's possible and making it a reality," Barton often emphasizes. His ability to foresee the potential of mobile technology and create a user-friendly app highlights the importance of vision and persistence.

Barton also stresses the importance of embracing change and being willing to pivot when necessary. "Success in technology requires continuous adaptation and a willingness to evolve," he advises aspiring entrepreneurs. His journey reflects the power of resilience and the impact of creating a product that meets a real need in the market.

Barton emphasizes that "game-changing innovations begin with mindset, not just creativity or risk-taking."

## A Legacy of Sound Innovation

Looking ahead, Barton remains committed to fostering innovation and supporting new ventures. He continues to inspire a new generation of entrepreneurs through speaking engagements and mentorship, sharing his experiences and insights on building successful tech companies. He advocates for what he calls "starting from zero thinking," which involves "questioning assumptions and breaking them down to basic truths."

## Conclusion

Chris Barton's story is a powerful example of how vision, resilience, and a commitment to solving real problems can lead to extraordinary success. From the early challenges of developing Shazam to building a transformative app that redefined music discovery, Barton's journey is marked by bold decisions and an unwavering dedication to his mission. His ability to navigate intense challenges and turn opportunities into transformative success has set a new standard in the tech industry. As Barton aptly puts it, "To succeed, entrepreneurs may need to generate hundreds or thousands of ideas, not just one."

# Yvon Chouinard

## Adventure Roots: From Maine to California

Born in Lewiston, Maine, in 1938, Yvon Chouinard moved with his family to Southern California at a young age. Surrounded by the rugged outdoors, he developed a passion for climbing, surfing, and exploring nature. This early love for adventure would become the foundation of his entrepreneurial journey.

## Forging Innovation

Chouinard's entrepreneurial journey began in the 1950s when he became an avid rock climber. Frustrated with the poor quality and environmental impact of the climbing gear available at the time, he decided to make his own. Teaching himself blacksmithing, he started forging pitons—metal spikes used in climbing—that were reusable and less damaging to rock faces. His innovative designs quickly gained a following among fellow climbers.

## From Tin Shed to Global Brand

In 1957, Chouinard Equipment was born. Operating out of the back of his car and a tin shed in Ventura, California, Chouinard crafted and sold his high-quality climbing gear. Recognizing a growing market for outdoor apparel, he expanded his business and founded Patagonia in 1973. Chouinard's vision for Patagonia was clear: to create high-performance clothing that was both stylish and environmentally responsible.

## Revolutionizing Outdoor Fashion

One of the most dramatic moments in Patagonia's early history came in 1972 when Chouinard introduced the first line of brightly colored rugby shirts for climbing. This bold move not only set a new trend in outdoor fashion but also marked Patagonia's entry into the apparel industry. The shirts were an instant success, and Chouinard realized the potential of combining functionality with style.

## Overcoming Business and Environmental Challenges

Building Patagonia was not without its challenges. In the late 1980s, Chouinard faced a significant crisis when his company's rapid growth began to strain both its finances and its environmental ethos. Faced with the possibility of bankruptcy, Chouinard made the difficult decision to downsize and refocus on Patagonia's core values.

One particularly intense period came in the early 1990s when Chouinard made the bold decision to switch all of Patagonia's cotton products to organic cotton. Despite the higher costs and logistical challenges, Chouinard's commitment to sustainability paid off. Patagonia's customers appreciated the company's environmental stance, reinforcing its reputation as a leader in sustainable business practices.

## Defying Convention

Patagonia's growth has been both steady and impactful. By the 2000s, the company had established itself as a leading brand in outdoor apparel, known for its high-quality products and strong environmental values. One of the most dramatic periods in Patagonia's history came in 2011 with the launch of the "Don't Buy This Jacket" campaign. This unconventional approach not only boosted Patagonia's sales but also solidified its position as a company committed to sustainability over profit.

## A Revolutionary Decision

In a move that shocked the business world, Yvon Chouinard announced in 2022 that he had transferred the ownership of Patagonia to a specially designed trust and a nonprofit organization. "Earth is now our only shareholder," Chouinard proclaimed. "I never wanted to be a businessman," he added. By placing Patagonia's voting stock into the Patagonia Purpose Trust and its non-voting stock into the Holdfast Collective, Chouinard ensured that the company's values would remain intact. This innovative structure means that every year, the money Patagonia makes after reinvesting in the business will be distributed as a dividend to help fight the environmental crisis. This bold decision reflects Chouinard's unwavering commitment to using business as a force for good.

## Leading with Purpose

Yvon Chouinard's journey offers valuable insights into the power of innovation, resilience, and a commitment to environmental stewardship. "Success is not just about growth; it's about doing the right thing for people and the planet," Chouinard often emphasizes. His ability to balance business success with environmental responsibility highlights the importance of values-driven leadership.

## Continuing the Mission

Looking ahead, Chouinard remains committed to advancing Patagonia's mission of environmental stewardship and responsible business practices. He envisions further growth and innovation, including expanding Patagonia's activism initiatives and promoting sustainable practices across the industry. His influence extends beyond Patagonia, actively supporting initiatives that promote environmental conservation, social justice, and sustainable business practices.

## Conclusion

Yvon Chouinard's journey with Patagonia is nothing short of revolutionary. From forging reusable pitons in a tin shed to placing his entire company into a trust to ensure environmental integrity, Chouinard has consistently defied business norms. His audacious moves, like the "Don't Buy This Jacket" campaign and the switch to organic cotton, highlight his unwavering commitment to sustainability. By making "Earth our only shareholder," Chouinard has redefined what it means to lead a purpose-driven business. His legacy is a testament to the power of innovation, resilience, and the profound impact of putting the planet first. Chouinard's story is a powerful reminder that true success is measured not just by profits but by the positive change we bring to the world.

# Julie Wainwright

## Reinventing Resilience and Luxury

Julie Wainwright's story is one of relentless perseverance and reinvention. Born in 1957 in Indiana, Wainwright's early career was rooted in the tech industry. After earning her degree in business from Purdue University, she climbed the ranks in Silicon Valley, eventually becoming the CEO of Reel.com and later, Pets.com.

## The Fall That Fueled a Rise

Wainwright's tenure at Pets.com ended in a very public and painful failure during the dot-com bust of 2000. The collapse of Pets.com, an online pet supply retailer, marked a significant setback. "It was a public failure, and I was devastated," Wainwright later reflected. This period forced her to reassess her career and future direction.

## Reinvention

In 2011, driven by a gap she identified in the luxury market, Wainwright founded The RealReal from her kitchen table. She envisioned a trusted online marketplace for authenticated, pre-owned luxury goods, combining her tech-savvy background with her love for fashion. "I wanted to create a business that was meaningful and had a positive impact," she said. The RealReal's commitment to authenticity, with a team of experts verifying every item, set it apart from other online marketplaces.

## Building Trust in a Skeptical Market

Launching The RealReal was not without its challenges. Wainwright faced significant skepticism from investors who doubted the viability of an online consignment model for luxury goods. However, her determination and clear vision prevailed. The company's innovative approach, combining online sales with physical consignment offices and retail stores, offered a seamless and trustworthy experience for buyers and sellers alike.

## Breaking Barriers and Setting Trends

The RealReal experienced rapid growth, particularly during the economic downturn when people sought additional income streams. This led to operational challenges, but Wainwright responded by investing in technology and expanding her team to maintain quality and customer experience. By 2015, The RealReal had millions of members and was generating significant revenue.

## IPO and Market Validation

One of the most significant milestones in The RealReal's history came in 2019 when the company went public, valued at nearly $2.4 billion. This success validated Wainwright's vision and hard work, marking a significant achievement in her entrepreneurial journey.

## Innovation and Authenticity

Julie Wainwright's journey offers profound insights into the power of resilience, innovation, and strategic thinking. "Success is about turning adversity into opportunity and staying true to your mission," she often emphasizes. Her ability to pivot from a high-profile failure to building a successful and impactful company underscores the importance of perseverance and adaptability.

Wainwright is also a strong advocate for sustainability in the fashion industry. "We're changing the way people think about luxury and consumption," she explains, highlighting The RealReal's role in promoting a circular economy. Her leadership has not only transformed the resale market but also influenced broader industry practices toward greater sustainability.

## Future Growth and Lasting Impact

Looking ahead, Wainwright remains committed to expanding The RealReal's mission of promoting sustainable fashion and providing a trusted marketplace for luxury goods. She envisions further growth through technology and innovation, aiming to enhance the customer experience and expand into new markets. Her dedication to sustainability continues to drive the company's mission, with plans to further integrate eco-friendly practices into every aspect of the business.

Wainwright's influence extends beyond The RealReal. She actively supports initiatives that promote female entrepreneurship and leadership, reflecting her belief in the power of business to drive positive change. Her journey has inspired a new generation of entrepreneurs to embrace resilience and innovation.

## Conclusion

Julie Wainwright's story is a powerful example of how resilience, innovation, and a commitment to meaningful impact can lead to extraordinary success. From the public fall of Pets.com to the triumph of The RealReal, Wainwright's journey is marked by bold decisions and an unwavering dedication to her vision. Her ability to navigate challenges and turn setbacks into opportunities has set a new standard in the fashion and technology industries. Julie Wainwright's legacy serves as an inspiring blueprint for overcoming adversity and achieving lasting success.

# Brian Chesky

## From Air Mattresses to IPO

Born on August 29, 1981, in Niskayuna, New York, Brian Chesky grew up in a supportive family that valued creativity and education. His parents, both social workers, instilled in him the importance of helping others and thinking outside the box. Chesky's early interests were diverse, ranging from sports to art, leading him to pursue industrial design at the Rhode Island School of Design (RISD). He earned a Bachelor of Fine Arts in Industrial Design in 2004, a decision that would be pivotal for his future in tech entrepreneurship.

## Turning a Rental Crisis into a Revolutionary Idea

Chesky's entrepreneurial journey began in 2007 when he moved to San Francisco with his college friend Joe Gebbia. Struggling to pay their rent, they noticed that a large design conference in the city had caused a shortage of hotel rooms. Seeing an opportunity, they decided to rent out air mattresses in their apartment and provide breakfast to guests. They created a simple website called "Air Bed & Breakfast" to attract attendees of the conference. This experiment was a success, marking the inception of what would become Airbnb.

Speaking about the early days of Airbnb, Brian Chesky shares: "Air Bed & Breakfast was just a way to keep paying rent before we came up with the big idea. We did not think Air Bed & Breakfast would be a company where 4 million people a night would use. Don't focus on the mountain top, focus on the first step. A lot of breakthrough ideas don't see breakthrough at the time, they just seem crazy."

## Building the Dream

In 2008, Chesky, Gebbia, and Nathan Blecharczyk, who joined as the third co-founder, officially launched Airbnb. The early days were fraught with challenges, including skepticism from investors who doubted that people would trust strangers enough to stay in their homes. Despite these obstacles, the trio was determined to make Airbnb work. They joined the Y Combinator startup accelerator program, which provided them with funding, mentorship, and invaluable advice.

One of the most dramatic moments in Airbnb's early days came during the 2008 Democratic National Convention in Denver. The founders created limited-edition cereal boxes called "Obama O's" and "Cap'n McCain's" to raise funds and gain publicity. This creative stunt generated media attention and much-needed revenue, helping Airbnb survive during a critical period.

## Navigating the Storm

Building Airbnb was not just about creating a platform for home rentals; it involved overcoming numerous obstacles and reshaping the way people thought about travel and accommodation. Trust was a major issue, as convincing people to open their homes to strangers was no easy task. Chesky and his team focused on building a strong community and ensuring safety through rigorous host and guest verification processes. Their efforts paid off as the platform gradually gained traction.

In addition to trust and safety issues, Airbnb faced legal and regulatory challenges in various cities around the world. Many local governments and hotel associations viewed Airbnb as a threat to traditional lodging businesses and sought to impose strict regulations. Chesky and his team had to navigate these complex legal landscapes, often engaging in negotiations and advocacy efforts to protect their business model.

One particularly intense period came in 2011 when a host's home was ransacked by a guest. This incident threatened to derail the company's growth. Chesky personally reached out to the affected host and took swift action to improve safety measures, including offering a $1 million host guarantee. This proactive response demonstrated Airbnb's commitment to its community and helped restore trust.

## The Path to Success

Airbnb's growth was rapid and transformative. By 2011, the platform had over one million nights booked and continued to expand globally. Chesky's focus on creating a user-friendly platform and fostering a sense of community among hosts and guests contributed to Airbnb's success.

One of the most dramatic periods in Airbnb's history came in 2020 with the onset of the COVID-19 pandemic. The global travel industry came to a standstill, and Airbnb faced significant financial challenges. Chesky made the difficult decision to lay off 25% of the company's workforce and pivot the business model to focus on long-term stays and local travel. This strategic shift helped Airbnb weather the crisis and emerge stronger.

In December 2020, Airbnb went public with one of the largest IPOs of the year, valuing the company at over $100 billion. This milestone validated Chesky's vision and hard work, marking a significant achievement in his entrepreneurial journey.

## Beyond Business

Brian Chesky's journey offers valuable insights into the power of creativity, resilience, and community. "Success is about creating something that people love and that makes a positive impact on the world," Chesky often emphasizes. His ability to identify a market need and build a platform that transformed the travel industry highlights the importance of innovation and staying true to one's values.

Chesky also stresses the importance of resilience and adaptability. "Building a business requires navigating challenges and being willing to pivot when necessary," he advises aspiring entrepreneurs. His journey reflects the power of perseverance and the impact of staying committed to one's vision, even in the face of adversity.

## Pioneering the Future of Travel and Belonging

Under Chesky's leadership, Airbnb continues to evolve, adapting to changing market dynamics and consumer preferences. The company has expanded beyond home rentals to include experiences, allowing users to book activities hosted by locals. Chesky remains dedicated to his vision of creating a world where anyone can belong anywhere. His legacy is marked by a transformative impact on the travel and hospitality industry, inspiring countless entrepreneurs to pursue their dreams with passion and perseverance.

Chesky's influence extends beyond Airbnb. He actively supports initiatives that promote entrepreneurship, creativity, and community building, reflecting his belief in the power of design and innovation to drive positive change. His work has inspired a new generation of entrepreneurs to pursue their visions and create impactful solutions.

## Conclusion

Chesky's approach to leadership, marked by empathy and a relentless focus on user experience, offers valuable lessons for aspiring entrepreneurs. He reminds us that success is not just about financial gain but about creating something that resonates with people and makes a positive impact. His insights into the loneliness of leadership and the importance of maintaining genuine human connections are particularly poignant, highlighting the often-overlooked personal struggles behind entrepreneurial success.

# Daniel Ek

## The Maestro Behind Spotify's Symphony

Born on February 21, 1983, in Stockholm, Sweden, Daniel Ek's journey to revolutionize the music industry started early. From building websites at 14 to earning more money than his parents, Ek's knack for technology was evident. His entrepreneurial spirit flourished, laying the foundation for his future groundbreaking ventures.

## Turning Piracy into Opportunity

Ek's frustration with the rampant piracy in the mid-2000s sparked his revolutionary idea. He envisioned a platform that not only provided legal access to music but also compensated artists fairly. "I wanted to build a service that was better than piracy and at the same time compensated the music industry," Ek once said. This vision was the seed that grew into Spotify.

## A Bold Vision with Bold Partners

In 2006, Ek joined forces with Martin Lorentzon, co-founder of TradeDoubler, to bring Spotify to life. Convincing record labels to license their music to a fledgling startup was a herculean task, but Ek's tenacity paid off. Spotify launched in Sweden in 2008, offering a freemium model that changed the music consumption landscape.

## Navigating Stormy Seas

Spotify's US launch was fraught with legal and financial hurdles. Ek's strategy and determination were crucial. "We knew that if we could make it in the US, we could make it anywhere," he remarked. By offering both a free ad-supported tier and a premium subscription, Spotify attracted a broad user base, turning skeptics into believers.

## Innovate or Die

Ek's leadership has been marked by relentless innovation. Personalized playlists, social sharing, and seamless integration with other digital services set Spotify apart. "We are in the business of making people happy through music," Ek emphasized. By 2020, Spotify boasted over 286 million active users across 79 countries, solidifying its global dominance.

## A Testament to Success

Spotify's valuation stands as a testament to Ek's visionary leadership. As of 2023, Spotify's market capitalization is approximately $70 billion, a remarkable achievement that underscores the platform's global impact and financial success.

## Wisdom from the Frontlines

Ek's journey offers profound lessons in resilience and vision. He stresses the importance of staying true to one's mission and adapting to change. "The only constant is change, and we have to embrace it," he advises. His commitment to improving the music industry has not only transformed listening habits but also created new opportunities for artists worldwide.

## Looking Ahead

Ek envisions Spotify as a comprehensive platform for all audio content, including podcasts and audiobooks. His dedication to innovation and user experience remains unwavering. "We are just getting started," he asserts, confident in Spotify's potential to shape the future of audio entertainment.

Beyond Spotify, Ek champions initiatives that foster entrepreneurship and technology education. His influence inspires a new generation of entrepreneurs to pursue their visions with passion and determination.

# Conclusion

Daniel Ek's story is a testament to how vision, resilience, and relentless innovation can lead to extraordinary success. From his early coding days in Stockholm to building Spotify into a global powerhouse, Ek's journey is marked by bold decisions and an unwavering commitment to transforming the music industry. His ability to navigate challenges and create a platform that benefits both users and artists has set a new standard in digital entertainment.

# Rachel Carlson

## From Boardroom to Blackboard

Born in 1988 in Boulder, Colorado, Carlson grew up in a family that valued education and public service. Her mother was a teacher, and her father was a professor, which instilled in her a deep appreciation for the transformative power of education. Carlson pursued her undergraduate studies at Stanford University and later earned an MBA from Stanford Graduate School of Business and a Master's in Education from the Stanford Graduate School of Education.

## The Aha! Moment

Carlson's entrepreneurial journey began with her firsthand experiences in education and her deep-seated belief in its potential to change lives. While working as an education policy advisor and later as a consultant at the White House and the Department of Education, Carlson observed the significant gaps in access to education for working adults. She realized that many employees, particularly those in low-wage jobs, lacked the opportunities to advance their education and careers due to financial and logistical barriers.

In 2015, Carlson, along with her co-founder Brittany Stich, envisioned a solution that would bridge this gap. They aimed to create a platform that would enable employers to offer education as a benefit to their employees, thus making higher education more accessible and affordable for working adults. This idea led to the creation of Guild Education.

## Navigating the Rapids of Fast Growth

In 2015, Carlson and Stich launched Guild Education with the mission to unlock opportunity for America's workforce through education and upskilling. They faced significant challenges in the early days, including skepticism from potential investors who doubted the feasibility of their model. Additionally, convincing employers to invest in their employees' education required overcoming traditional notions about corporate benefits.

One of the most dramatic moments in Guild Education's early history came when Carlson and her team successfully partnered with major corporations like Chipotle and Walmart. These partnerships validated Guild's model and demonstrated the demand for innovative educational benefits. The success of these partnerships provided the momentum needed to scale the platform and attract additional corporate partners.

## Hitting Unicorn Status

Building Guild Education was not without its challenges. Carlson faced significant obstacles, including navigating the complexities of integrating educational programs with corporate benefit structures and ensuring the quality and relevance of the educational offerings. Additionally, she had to address the financial constraints faced by many working adults, ensuring that the programs offered were both affordable and accessible.

One particularly intense period came in 2018 when Guild Education experienced rapid growth, leading to operational challenges. The company struggled to keep up with the demand from both employers and employees, putting a strain on its resources. Carlson responded by investing in technology and expanding her team, ensuring that Guild could scale effectively while maintaining high standards of service and support.

## From Humble Beginnings to High Impact

Guild Education's growth has been rapid and transformative. By 2020, the company had partnered with numerous Fortune 500 companies and provided educational opportunities to thousands of employees. Carlson's focus on creating a user-friendly platform and fostering strong partnerships with employers and educational institutions has driven significant impact and loyalty.

One of the most dramatic periods in Guild Education's history came in 2021 when the company achieved unicorn status, with a valuation exceeding $1 billion. This milestone validated Carlson's vision and hard work, marking a significant achievement in her entrepreneurial journey. The recognition also underscored the growing importance of education as a critical component of corporate benefits.

## Eyes on the Horizon

Rachel Carlson's journey offers valuable insights into the power of vision, resilience, and strategic thinking. "Success is about creating opportunities that empower people and make a real difference in their lives," Carlson often emphasizes. Her ability to identify a critical need in the education sector and build a platform that bridges the gap between employers and employees highlights the importance of innovation and perseverance.

Carlson also stresses the importance of empathy and understanding. "Building a successful business requires listening to the needs of your users and creating solutions that address their challenges," she advises aspiring entrepreneurs. Her journey reflects the power of resilience and the impact of creating a business that prioritizes accessibility and empowerment.

## Pearls of Wisdom

Looking ahead, Carlson remains committed to advancing Guild Education's mission of democratizing education and providing opportunities for lifelong learning. She envisions further growth and innovation, including expanding the company's educational offerings and enhancing its technology platform to provide even more personalized and effective learning experiences.

Carlson's influence extends beyond Guild Education. She actively supports initiatives that promote education and workforce development, reflecting her belief in the power of education to drive positive change. Her work has inspired a new generation of entrepreneurs to pursue their visions and create impactful solutions in the education sector.

## Conclusion

Rachel Carlson's journey is a testament to how vision, resilience, and a commitment to empowerment can redefine industries and change lives. From her early experiences to building Guild Education into a groundbreaking platform, Carlson has shown that with determination and a clear mission, significant impact is possible. Her story inspires others to embrace challenges and pursue their visions with passion and dedication.

# Brian Halligan

## The Mastermind Behind the Inbound Revolution

### From Gadgets to Game-Changer

Born on September 21, 1967, in Westwood, Massachusetts, Brian Halligan demonstrated an early knack for technology. He pursued engineering at the University of Vermont, setting the stage for his future as a tech entrepreneur. His early career in the tech industry, including a stint at PTC, honed his skills and prepared him for his groundbreaking work in digital marketing.

### A Lightbulb Moment

Halligan's journey took a pivotal turn at MIT, where he earned an MBA and met Dharmesh Shah. The two shared a frustration with traditional marketing methods that felt intrusive and outdated. They saw consumers turning to the internet for product research, prompting them to develop a new marketing strategy that leveraged this shift.

## Redefining the Rules

In 2006, Halligan and Shah founded HubSpot, aiming to revolutionize how businesses attract, engage, and delight customers. They coined the term "inbound marketing," focusing on creating valuable content to draw customers in. HubSpot's platform integrates various digital marketing tools, simplifying inbound marketing for businesses of all sizes. Initially targeting mainstream sales and marketing professionals rather than CEOs, HubSpot successfully broadened its appeal.

## Rocketing to Success

Under Halligan's leadership, HubSpot rapidly evolved from a startup to a global marketing software leader. A major milestone was HubSpot's IPO in 2014, which valued the company at nearly $1 billion. This achievement underscored Halligan's vision and the company's impact on the marketing industry. Early startup metrics focused on visitors, leads, and customers, but later evolved to include churn, cost to acquire a customer, and total lifetime value of a customer, reflecting a more mature approach to growth.

## HubSpot's Secret Sauce

A significant part of HubSpot's success lies in its vibrant company culture. Halligan emphasizes a positive, inclusive work environment that fosters innovation and attracts top talent. HubSpot conducts rigorous 360 reviews annually to identify strengths and areas for improvement, emphasizing continuous personal and professional development. This approach has earned HubSpot numerous accolades, including recognition as one of the best places to work by Glassdoor.

## Navigating the Rough

Building HubSpot wasn't without hurdles. The company faced fierce competition and the challenge of educating the market about inbound marketing's benefits. Transitioning from a founder's role as a control freak to empowering others can be challenging during company growth. Halligan's strategic vision and commitment to innovation helped HubSpot maintain its edge and ensure sustainable growth. His decision to relinquish the Head of Product role when feedback indicated it wasn't his strength highlights his self-awareness and humility—traits ingrained in HubSpot's culture and influencing hiring decisions.

## Thought Leader and Philanthropist

Halligan is also a respected thought leader. He has co-authored several influential books on inbound marketing and sales, including "Inbound Marketing: Get Found Using Google, Social Media, and Blogs." His philanthropic efforts support entrepreneurship, education, and innovation, reflecting his belief in business as a force for good.

## Pioneering New Frontiers

Halligan continues to drive HubSpot's mission of helping businesses grow better. He is keen on leveraging emerging technologies like artificial intelligence and machine learning to enhance marketing strategies. His influence extends beyond HubSpot, inspiring a new generation of entrepreneurs and marketers.

## Conclusion

Brian Halligan's journey is a testament to the power of visionary leadership, constant innovation, and unwavering commitment to customer success. From his early engineering days to co-founding and guiding HubSpot, Halligan has consistently pushed the boundaries of marketing. His story is one of transformation and inspiration, illustrating that with the right mindset and approach, any obstacle can be overcome, and significant, lasting change can be achieved. His legacy is a powerful reminder that determination and a clear vision can lead to extraordinary accomplishments.

# Joachim Sauter & Pavel Mayer

## The Billion Dollar Code

Joachim Sauter was born in 1959 in Ulm, Germany, and Pavel Mayer was born in 1961 in Prague, Czech Republic. Both grew up in environments that encouraged intellectual curiosity and a love for technology. Sauter pursued a background in design and media art, while Mayer focused on computer science and software development. Their diverse backgrounds would later converge to create a revolutionary impact in the world of digital art and interactive media.

## Terravision: A Vision Ahead of Its Time

In the early 1990s, Sauter and Mayer, alongside Carsten Schlüter and Juri Müller, developed Terravision. This innovative software allowed users to view satellite imagery of the Earth in a 3D environment, predating Google Earth by over a decade. Despite their revolutionary work, they struggled to monetize Terravision but garnered significant attention from tech enthusiasts and professionals.

## A Profound Technological Advance

Terravision's technology was based on sophisticated algorithms that processed and rendered satellite imagery in real-time, allowing users to explore the Earth from a virtual perspective. This capability was revolutionary, laying the groundwork for future digital globe applications. Terravision provided an intuitive interface for visualizing complex data sets, setting a new standard for interactive media and geographical visualization.

## The Google Earth Controversy

Terravision's groundbreaking concept caught the eye of Google executives. In 2003, Schlüter and Müller presented Terravision at a tech conference in California, where several Google execs were present. The following year, Google acquired Keyhole, Inc., which had developed similar software. In 2005, Google Earth was launched, bearing striking resemblances to Terravision.

## Legal Battle and Triumph

Feeling their idea was stolen, Schlüter and Müller sued Google in 2014 for patent infringement. The lawsuit highlighted the David vs. Goliath dynamic between small innovators and tech giants. After a protracted legal battle, a German court ruled in favor of Schlüter and Müller in 2017, awarding them €140 million in damages. This landmark case underscored the importance of intellectual property protection for innovators and the vulnerabilities they face against larger corporations.

## Reflections and Lessons

The saga of Terravision vs. Google Earth serves as a cautionary tale about the importance of protecting intellectual property. Sauter and Mayer's journey emphasizes the need for innovators to secure patents and remain vigilant about sharing their ideas. Their story is a testament to perseverance and the impact of standing up for one's creative rights.

## Conclusion

Despite the challenges, Sauter and Mayer's work with ART+COM and their role in the Terravision project have left an indelible mark on the digital art and technology landscape. They continue to inspire a new generation of artists and technologists to explore the intersection of their fields, pushing the boundaries of what is possible in interactive media.

Their story is a call to action for innovators everywhere: protect your ideas, persist through challenges, and never underestimate the impact of your work. In doing so, you may just transform the world, one breakthrough at a time.

# Sara Blakely

## Reinventing Shapewear

### Early Life and the Drive for Reinvention

Born in 1971 in Clearwater, Florida, Blakely grew up in a supportive family that encouraged creativity and perseverance. Her father, an attorney, and her mother, an artist, instilled in her the importance of persistence and thinking outside the box. These lessons would become crucial as Blakely embarked on her entrepreneurial journey.

### A Wardrobe Dilemma Sparks Genius

Blakely's entrepreneurial journey began with a personal frustration. In the late 1990s, while preparing for a party, she struggled to find a pair of pantyhose that wouldn't show through her cream-colored pants. Dissatisfied with the available options, she cut the feet off a pair of control-top pantyhose, creating a makeshift solution that smoothed her figure without visible seams. This simple but effective hack sparked an idea: why not create a new kind of shapewear that offered the same benefits without the drawbacks of traditional products?

Determined to bring her idea to life, Blakely spent the next two years researching, designing, and developing a prototype. She invested her entire savings of $5,000 and began the arduous process of finding a manufacturer willing to produce her unique product. Despite numerous rejections and setbacks, Blakely's persistence paid off when she finally secured a manufacturer in North Carolina.

## Going All In

In 2000, Blakely officially launched Spanx with the goal of offering women a more comfortable and effective solution for shaping their bodies. She handled every aspect of the business herself, from designing the packaging to writing the patent application. Blakely's innovative approach and dedication to quality set Spanx apart from other shapewear products on the market.

One of the most dramatic moments in Spanx's early history came when Blakely managed to secure a meeting with a buyer at Neiman Marcus. In a bold move, she demonstrated her product by changing into a pair of Spanx in the bathroom and showing the buyer the difference it made. This impromptu demonstration convinced Neiman Marcus to carry Spanx, marking a significant breakthrough for the brand.

## Rolling with the Punches

Building Spanx was not without its challenges. Blakely faced significant obstacles, including skepticism from industry insiders who doubted the viability of her product. Additionally, she had to navigate the complexities of scaling a business with limited resources and experience. Blakely's unyielding determination and willingness to learn on the fly were critical in overcoming these challenges.

One particularly intense period came when Blakely decided to take a risk by sending a basket of Spanx products to Oprah Winfrey's stylist. This bold move paid off when Oprah named Spanx her "Favorite Product of the Year" in 2000. The endorsement catapulted Spanx into the national spotlight, driving massive demand and establishing the brand as a household name.

## Skyrocketing Success

Spanx's growth was rapid and transformative. By 2001, the company's products were being sold in major department stores across the United States. Blakely's focus on creating high-quality, innovative shapewear resonated with women of all ages, driving significant sales and customer loyalty.

One of the most dramatic periods in Spanx's history came in 2012 when Forbes named Blakely the youngest self-made female billionaire. This milestone was a testament to Blakely's vision and hard work, highlighting the impact of Spanx on the fashion industry. Her journey from a struggling entrepreneur to a billionaire businesswoman inspired countless others to pursue their own entrepreneurial dreams.

## Shapewear Revolution

Sara Blakely's journey offers valuable insights into the power of innovation, resilience, and strategic thinking. "Success is about finding a problem and solving it in a way that nobody else has," Blakely often emphasizes. Her ability to identify a gap in the market and create a product that addressed a real need highlights the importance of innovation and perseverance.

Blakely also stresses the importance of authenticity and believing in oneself. "Building a successful business requires staying true to your vision and never giving up, even when faced with obstacles," she advises aspiring entrepreneurs. Her journey reflects the power of resilience and the impact of creating a business that prioritizes quality and customer satisfaction.

## Vision Forward

Looking ahead, Blakely remains committed to advancing Spanx's mission of empowering women through innovative shapewear and apparel. She envisions further growth and innovation, including expanding the company's product offerings and enhancing its digital presence to reach a global audience.

Blakely's influence extends beyond Spanx. She actively supports initiatives that promote female entrepreneurship and empowerment, reflecting her belief in the power of business to drive positive change. Her work has inspired a new generation of female entrepreneurs to pursue their visions and create impactful solutions in their industries.

## Conclusion

Sara Blakely's story is a powerful example of how innovation, resilience, and a commitment to quality can lead to extraordinary success. From her early challenges in launching Spanx to building a revolutionary brand that redefined shapewear, Blakely's journey is marked by bold decisions and unwavering dedication to her vision. Her ability to navigate intense challenges and turn opportunities into remarkable achievements has set a new standard in the fashion industry. Blakely's journey serves as an inspiring reminder that with determination and a clear mission, any obstacle can be overcome, turning simple ideas into billion-dollar realities.

# Neil Patel

## Digital Marketing Dynamo Redefining Success

B orn on April 24, 1985, in London, England, Neil Patel moved to Orange County, California, at a young age. Raised by immigrant parents who ran their own businesses, Patel was instilled with a strong work ethic and an entrepreneurial spirit from an early age.

His journey into the world of digital marketing began in high school when he started selling CDs and black boxes, igniting his passion for business and technology. At 16, Neil created his first website and, after being ripped off by marketing firms, he was compelled to learn marketing on his own.

Demonstrating an early knack for academics, Neil was able to get a head start in college while still in high school. With the help of his sister, he took general education courses at Cypress Community College. This initiative allowed him to accelerate his educational journey and gain valuable knowledge and skills that would later benefit his entrepreneurial endeavors.

## Turning Frustration into Innovation

Neil's entrepreneurial journey took off in high school with his first online venture selling car parts. Realizing the need for effective marketing to attract customers, he dove into the world of digital marketing, learning SEO, PPC advertising, and other strategies. His determination to master these skills led him to launch Advantage Consulting Services in 2001, where he quickly gained recognition for driving traffic and improving search rankings for his clients.

## Visualizing Success

In 2006, Patel co-founded Crazy Egg with Hiten Shah, offering visual analytics through heatmaps to help businesses optimize their websites. Following this success, they launched KISSmetrics in 2008, focusing on customer analytics and conversion tracking. These ventures solidified Patel's reputation as a digital marketing expert, providing valuable tools for businesses to enhance user engagement and performance.

## Crafting a Marketing Powerhouse

Building on his experience, Patel founded Neil Patel Digital in 2017, a comprehensive digital marketing agency designed to help businesses grow through effective online strategies. Offering services like SEO, content marketing, social media marketing, and conversion rate optimization, the agency quickly became a leading force in the industry. Patel's personal brand, established through his extensive blogging and public speaking, provided a solid foundation for the agency's success. Neil's blog, NeilPatel.com, attracts 2.3 million visitors monthly, showcasing his expertise in generating traffic and engaging content.

Neil is a prolific blogger, maintaining a systematic approach to content creation supported by an editorial team and a content calendar. His blog is known for its valuable insights, tips, and strategies for digital marketers, consistently driving traffic and sparking conversation.

## Overcoming Adversity

Patel's journey was not without challenges. Intense competition from established marketing agencies and the ever-evolving digital landscape posed significant obstacles. Additionally, scaling his service-based business while maintaining high-quality standards required meticulous planning and execution. Despite these challenges, Patel's commitment to innovation and customer satisfaction helped him navigate these hurdles successfully.

## Democratizing SEO for All

In 2017, Patel acquired Ubersuggest, an SEO tool providing keyword suggestions, content ideas, and backlink data. His vision was to make SEO accessible to everyone, regardless of budget, by offering a powerful and affordable tool. Ubersuggest has since helped countless businesses improve their online presence, aligning with Patel's mission to democratize digital marketing.

## Giving Back to the Community

Beyond his business ventures, Neil Patel is passionate about giving back. He actively supports charitable organizations and initiatives promoting education and entrepreneurship. As a mentor, he shares his experiences and insights with aspiring entrepreneurs, helping them navigate their own paths to success. Recognized for his contributions,

Neil was named one of the top 100 entrepreneurs under 30 by President Barack Obama and one of the top 100 entrepreneurs under 35 by the United Nations, receiving Congressional Recognition from the U.S. House of Representatives.

## Blogging Brilliance

Neil co-authored the bestselling book "Hustle: The Power to Charge Your Life with Money, Meaning, and Momentum," which provides insights into achieving success through redefining hustle. He also hosts a daily podcast called "Marketing School" with Eric Siu, which receives one million listens per month and covers a variety of digital marketing topics in concise episodes.

Neil's blog is a cornerstone of his digital marketing influence. With an editorial team and a content calendar, he consistently publishes engaging and traffic-driving content. His systematic approach ensures his blog remains a go-to resource for digital marketers worldwide.

## Trusted by the Best

Neil's impressive client roster includes high-profile brands like Amazon, eBay, Google, Salesforce, NBC, General Motors, Hewlett Packard, and Viacom. He has also delivered presentations to major companies like Facebook and Thomson Reuters. His influence extends beyond his agency, as he actively supports initiatives that promote entrepreneurship, education, and technology adoption, reflecting his belief in the power of knowledge and innovation to drive positive change.

## The Future of Digital Marketing

Looking ahead, Patel remains committed to advancing digital marketing through innovation. He envisions a future where data-driven insights and personalized marketing strategies become the norm, leveraging artificial intelligence and machine learning to enhance marketing effectiveness. Patel's focus includes developing new tools and resources to support businesses in their marketing efforts.

## Conclusion

Neil Patel's evolution from a teenage tech enthusiast to a world-renowned digital marketing expert underscores the power of innovation, perseverance, and a relentless focus on delivering value. His pioneering work with Crazy Egg, KISSmetrics, and Neil Patel Digital has not only redefined the digital marketing landscape but also empowered countless businesses to succeed online. Patel's narrative is a compelling testament to the impact of continuous learning, strategic thinking, and an unwavering dedication to one's goals. It reminds us that with the right mindset and approach, significant challenges can be transformed into opportunities, paving the way for lasting success and influence.

# Benjamin Francis

## From Garage Startup to Fitness Empire

Born in 1992 in Bromsgrove, England, Benjamin Francis always had a passion for fitness and technology. This unique combination of interests set the stage for what would become one of the most transformative brands in the fitness industry. As a student at Aston University, Ben juggled his academic responsibilities with a part-time job as a pizza delivery driver. However, his entrepreneurial spirit was the driving force behind his ambition.

In 2012, at just 19 years old, Ben embarked on his entrepreneurial journey from his parents' garage. With a modest investment of £1,000, a sewing machine, and a screen printer, he began creating fitness apparel. His vision was revolutionary yet straightforward: to provide stylish, high-quality gym wear that fitness enthusiasts would love.

## The Spark That Ignited Gymshark

The fitness apparel market was dominated by big brands, but Ben saw an opportunity to offer affordable, stylish gym wear tailored specifically for young fitness enthusiasts. Leveraging his background in technology, he began learning how to design and sew his own gym wear. Initially, Gymshark focused on selling supplements, but Ben quickly realized there was a greater demand for innovative fitness apparel. This pivotal realization set Gymshark on its path to success.

Ben's strategy was to harness the power of social media and influencer marketing, which were still in their infancy at the time. He reached out to popular fitness influencers on YouTube and Instagram, sending them Gymshark products. This move paid off massively, as these influencers embraced the brand, showcasing it to millions of followers.

## Turning Points and Triumphs

The early days of Gymshark were marked by relentless hustle and dedication. Ben juggled his university studies, a part-time job, and the growing demands of his new business. One of Gymshark's first big breaks came in 2013 when the brand attended the BodyPower Expo in Birmingham. Ben and his team, which included his school friend Lewis Morgan, sold out their entire stock of Luxe tracksuits within just a few hours. This success validated their efforts and confirmed that Gymshark had struck a chord with the fitness community.

In one particularly memorable incident, Ben recounted how a simple Facebook post announcing the store reopening led to an overwhelming influx of orders. "In the first 30 minutes after turning the website back on, we'd sold more Gymshark product than in our entire history. We'd completely sold out of everything we had."

## Navigating Challenges

Building Gymshark into a global brand was not without its challenges. One significant obstacle was managing rapid growth. The demand for Gymshark products often outstripped supply, leading to stock shortages and logistical challenges. However, Ben's ability to adapt and find solutions helped the brand navigate these hurdles.

Another challenge was maintaining the brand's authenticity and connection with its audience. As Gymshark grew, it became crucial to stay true to its roots and continue engaging with the fitness community. Ben achieved this by maintaining a strong presence on social media and staying personally involved in the brand's marketing efforts.

One particularly intense period came in 2015 when Gymshark experienced severe website crashes during major sales events, resulting in lost revenue and frustrated customers. Determined to resolve these issues, Ben invested in robust e-commerce infrastructure and hired a dedicated tech team to ensure that the website could handle high traffic volumes. This investment paid off, as Gymshark continued to grow and improve its customer experience.

## Achieving Unprecedented Success

Gymshark's growth has been nothing short of meteoric. By 2020, the brand was valued at over £1 billion, making it one of the fastest-growing fitness apparel companies in the world. This success is a testament to Ben's vision and his ability to build a brand that resonates deeply with its audience.

One of the most notable milestones in Gymshark's journey came in August 2020, when the company secured a £200 million investment from General Atlantic, a leading global growth equity firm. This investment not only validated Gymshark's business model but also provided the resources needed to fuel further expansion.

## Visionary Insights

Ben Francis's journey offers valuable insights into the power of innovation, resilience, and community building. "Success is about creating products that people love and building a community around your brand," Francis often emphasizes. His ability to identify a market need and create a brand that resonates with fitness enthusiasts highlights the importance of understanding and engaging with your target audience.

Ben also highlights the importance of staying true to one's vision and values. "Building a successful brand requires a relentless focus on quality and a commitment to your customers," he advises aspiring entrepreneurs. His journey reflects the power of authenticity and the impact of creating a brand that resonates on a personal level.

## A Future Built on Innovation and Community

Looking ahead, Gymshark remains committed to advancing the fitness industry and creating innovative products that inspire and empower people. The company continues to explore new designs and technologies, pushing the boundaries of what is possible in fitness apparel.

Ben Francis's influence extends beyond Gymshark. He actively supports initiatives that promote entrepreneurship and fitness, reflecting his belief in the power of business and community to drive positive change. His work has inspired a new generation of entrepreneurs to pursue their passions and create brands that make a difference.

## Conclusion

As Gymshark continues to grow and evolve, Ben's commitment to quality, community, and innovation remains at the core of the brand. His story serves as an inspiring reminder that with determination and a clear mission, any obstacle can be overcome, and dreams can become reality. Ben Francis's journey is a testament to the impact of combining passion with perseverance, and his legacy will undoubtedly inspire future generations to pursue their own extraordinary success.

# Tony Xu

## From Takeout to Triumph

Born in Nanjing, China, in 1985, Tony Xu moved to the United States with his family at the age of five. Settling in Champaign, Illinois, Xu's parents juggled multiple jobs to make ends meet. This immigrant experience instilled in him a profound appreciation for hard work and opportunity. His father was a software engineer, and his mother worked in various roles, including running her own medical clinic, demonstrating resilience and entrepreneurship that deeply influenced Xu's future endeavors.

## Bootstrapping Beginnings

While studying at Stanford University, Xu encountered the significant challenges faced by small businesses, particularly local restaurants, in delivering food efficiently to customers. This observation, coupled with his passion for technology, led him to envision a platform that could bridge this gap. Together with his Stanford classmates Andy Fang and Stanley Tang, Xu launched PaloAltoDelivery.com in 2013, a service connecting local restaurants with customers through a user-friendly app. The initial success validated their idea, leading to the rebranding and expansion of the service as DoorDash.

## Financial Hurdles and Strategic Moves

Xu and his co-founders officially founded DoorDash in 2013, aiming to create a scalable food delivery platform. The early days were challenging, with Xu personally taking on multiple roles, from making deliveries to signing up restaurants. Their dedication paid off, and the company's focus on leveraging technology to optimize delivery routes and enhance customer experience quickly gained traction.

## Navigating Challenges and Scaling Heights

Building DoorDash involved overcoming numerous obstacles, including intense competition from established players like UberEats and GrubHub, and navigating regulatory hurdles. One particularly challenging period came in 2016 when DoorDash faced criticism over its tipping policy, leading to public backlash and legal scrutiny. Xu responded by overhauling the tipping structure, increasing transparency, and ensuring fair compensation for delivery drivers. This crisis tested Xu's leadership but ultimately strengthened DoorDash's commitment to its drivers and customers.

## From Startup to Market Leader

DoorDash's growth has been nothing short of extraordinary. By 2020, the company had become the market leader in the U.S. food delivery industry, capturing nearly 50% of the market share. A notable milestone was its initial public offering (IPO) in December 2020, valuing the company at over $70 billion. This success highlighted Xu's vision and leadership, transforming DoorDash from a startup into a dominant force in the food delivery sector.

## Visionary Insights:

Tony Xu's journey offers valuable insights into the power of resilience, innovation, and strategic thinking. "I'd rather die chasing excellence than live being mediocre," Xu often emphasizes. His ability to identify a market need and build a platform that bridges the gap between businesses and consumers underscores the importance of addressing customer pain points and creating value. "Success is about solving real problems and creating value for both customers and partners," he notes, highlighting the need for a customer-centric approach in business.

## Pioneering the Future

Looking ahead, Xu remains focused on expanding DoorDash's mission of empowering local economies. He envisions further growth through innovation, including extending DoorDash's offerings to include grocery delivery and other local services. Xu's commitment to leveraging technology to improve logistics and customer experience continues to drive DoorDash's evolution. "DoorDash really is a reflection of all of the local communities that sustain us," Xu says, emphasizing the company's deep connection with local businesses and its role in fostering equitable opportunities.

## Conclusion

Beyond DoorDash, Xu actively supports initiatives that promote entrepreneurship and innovation, reflecting his belief in the power of technology to drive positive change. His journey inspires a new generation of entrepreneurs to pursue their visions and create impactful solutions. Xu's story serves as a powerful reminder that with determination, resilience, and a clear mission, any obstacle can be overcome, setting new standards in the tech and delivery industries.

# Arianna Huffington

## Redefining Media and Wellness with The Huffington Post and Thrive Global

### Early Life and the Drive for Influence

Born in Athens, Greece, in 1950, Huffington moved to the United Kingdom at the age of 16 to attend Cambridge University. There, she became the first foreign and third female president of the Cambridge Union, showcasing her early leadership skills and passion for debate and communication. This early success set the stage for her future endeavors in media and beyond.

### From Author to Media Mogul

Huffington's career began in the world of writing and public speaking. She authored several books and gained recognition for her political commentary and syndicated column. However, her entrepreneurial journey took a significant turn in 2005 when she co-founded The Huffington Post, an online news and blog site, with Kenneth Lerer, Jonah Peretti, and Andrew Breitbart. The idea was to create a platform that combined traditional news reporting with a diverse range of voices and opinions, leveraging the burgeoning power of the internet to democratize media.

## A Digital Media Revolution

In 2005, The Huffington Post was launched as a digital-first media outlet that offered a mix of news, blogs, and original content. Huffington's vision was to provide a platform that could engage readers with a wide array of topics, from politics and business to lifestyle and entertainment. The Huffington Post quickly gained traction for its unique blend of content and its willingness to publish a variety of perspectives.

One of the most dramatic moments in The Huffington Post's early history came during the 2008 U.S. presidential election. The site's comprehensive and dynamic coverage, combined with its interactive features, significantly increased its readership. The Huffington Post's innovative approach to online journalism, including the use of social media and reader engagement, helped it become a major player in the media landscape.

## Navigating the Digital Frontier

Building The Huffington Post was not without its challenges. Huffington faced significant obstacles, including skepticism from traditional media outlets and the difficulties of monetizing online content. Additionally, she had to navigate the rapid changes in the digital media landscape, which required constant innovation and adaptation.

One particularly intense period came in 2011 when AOL acquired The Huffington Post for $315 million. This acquisition was a significant milestone but also brought new challenges, such as integrating with a larger corporate structure while maintaining the site's editorial independence. Huffington took on the role of president and editor-in-chief of The Huffington Post Media Group, overseeing not only the original site but also AOL's other media properties. Her leadership during this transition was crucial in maintaining the integrity and growth of the brand.

## Rising Above

The Huffington Post's growth was rapid and transformative. By 2012, it had become one of the most visited news sites in the world, with millions of unique visitors each month. Huffington's focus on creating engaging, diverse content and leveraging the power of social media played a key role in this success.

One of the most dramatic periods in The Huffington Post's history came in 2012 when it won the Pulitzer Prize for national reporting, becoming the first digital media outlet to receive this prestigious award. This recognition validated Huffington's vision and highlighted the impact of The Huffington Post on the journalism industry.

## Thrive Global

After leaving The Huffington Post in 2016, Huffington founded Thrive Global, a company focused on ending the stress and burnout epidemic and promoting wellness and productivity. Inspired by her personal experiences with burnout, Huffington aimed to change the way people work and live by providing science-based solutions to improve well-being.

Thrive Global's approach combines technology, storytelling, and practical tools to help individuals and organizations enhance their well-being and performance. Under Huffington's leadership, Thrive

Global has partnered with major corporations to integrate wellness into their cultures and has expanded its reach globally.

## Beyond Traditional Success

Arianna Huffington's journey offers valuable insights into the power of resilience, innovation, and purpose-driven leadership. "Success is not just about money or status, but about living a life true to your values," Huffington often emphasizes. Her ability to pioneer new frontiers in digital media and wellness highlights the importance of vision and adaptability.

Huffington also stresses the importance of well-being and balance. "We need to redefine success beyond the traditional metrics of money and power to include well-being, wisdom, and wonder," she advises. Her journey reflects the power of resilience and the impact of prioritizing holistic success.

## The Future and Legacy

Looking ahead, Huffington remains committed to advancing Thrive Global's mission of improving well-being and performance. She envisions further growth and innovation, including expanding the company's product offerings and leveraging technology to provide personalized wellness solutions.

Huffington's influence extends beyond her ventures. She actively supports initiatives that promote women's leadership, mental health, and education, reflecting her belief in the power of well-being to drive positive change. Her work has inspired a new generation of leaders to prioritize wellness and create impactful solutions.

# Conclusion

Arianna Huffington's journey is a testament to the transformative power of resilience and vision. From the bustling newsrooms of The Huffington Post to the wellness-focused mission of Thrive Global, her story is a vivid illustration of how innovation, tenacity, and a commitment to well-being can create lasting impact. Huffington's legacy is not just in the media platforms she built or the wellness initiatives she spearheaded but in the countless individuals she has inspired to lead healthier, more balanced lives. As she continues to drive forward with new initiatives, her journey underscores the importance of embracing change, prioritizing personal well-being, and inspiring future generations to redefine success on their terms.

# Jimmy Donaldson

## Mastering the Art of Viral Content with MrBeast

### Early Life and the Drive for Creativity

Born in 1998 in Greenville, North Carolina, Donaldson showed an early interest in digital media and the internet. As a child, he spent countless hours watching YouTube videos and dreaming of creating his own. This passion for video content and an entrepreneurial spirit would later define his career.

### Pioneering Philanthropy in Content Creation

Donaldson's entrepreneurial journey began at the age of 13 when he started his first YouTube channel in 2011. Under the username "MrBeast6000," he initially focused on Let's Play videos and other gaming content. However, his channel saw limited growth. Determined to succeed, Donaldson spent years studying the platform's algorithm and trends, seeking to understand what made certain videos go viral.

In 2017, Donaldson's hard work paid off when he posted a video of himself counting to 100,000, a task that took him over 40 hours to complete. The video quickly went viral, attracting millions of views and propelling MrBeast into the YouTube spotlight. This breakthrough moment sparked the idea for a new type of content—extreme challenges and philanthropy-based videos that were designed to captivate audiences and push the boundaries of what was possible on YouTube.

## Pushing the Limits of Creativity

With a clear vision and a newfound audience, Donaldson focused on creating content that combined outrageous stunts, heartwarming philanthropy, and innovative challenges. He reinvested all his earnings back into his videos, continually raising the stakes and production quality. His unique approach resonated with viewers, driving rapid growth and establishing MrBeast as a leading YouTube channel.

One of the most dramatic moments in MrBeast's early history came when Donaldson launched a series of videos where he gave away large sums of money to strangers and friends. These videos not only showcased his generosity but also tapped into the viral nature of social media, where acts of kindness and extreme challenges quickly spread.

## Building Empires

Building MrBeast was not without its challenges. Donaldson faced significant obstacles, including the constant pressure to innovate and outdo his previous videos. The high cost of producing such elaborate content required meticulous planning and financial management. Additionally, the physical and mental toll of creating extreme challenge videos pushed Donaldson and his team to their limits.

One particularly intense period came in 2019 when Donaldson decided to launch the #TeamTrees campaign, aiming to raise $20 million to plant 20 million trees by the end of the year. Partnering with the Arbor Day Foundation, Donaldson leveraged his platform and connections within the YouTube community to promote the initiative. The campaign quickly went viral, surpassing its goal and raising over $23 million. This effort showcased Donaldson's ability to mobilize his audience for a greater cause and demonstrated the potential of digital platforms to drive real-world impact.

Jimmy has successfully expanded his brand beyond YouTube, launching successful ventures such as the MrBeast Burger chain, Feastables chocolate company and engaging in significant environmental initiatives like Team Trees and Team Seas.

## From Small Beginnings to Internet Stardom

MrBeast's growth has been rapid and transformative. By 2020, the channel had amassed tens of millions of subscribers and billions of views, making it one of the most popular on YouTube. Donaldson's focus on reinvestment and constant innovation ensured that his content remained fresh and engaging.

One of the most dramatic periods in MrBeast's history came in 2021 when Donaldson launched MrBeast Burger, a virtual restaurant chain. By partnering with local restaurants across the United States, he was able to offer a menu of branded burgers and fries available for delivery through popular apps. This venture was a massive success, demonstrating Donaldson's ability to leverage his digital fame into real-world business opportunities.

## Bold Stunts and Bigger Ideas

Jimmy Donaldson's journey offers valuable insights into the power of creativity, resilience, and strategic thinking. "Success on YouTube isn't just about going viral; it's about understanding your audience and constantly pushing the envelope," Donaldson often emphasizes. His ability to innovate and create content that resonates deeply with viewers highlights the importance of understanding and engaging with your audience.

Donaldson also stresses the importance of reinvestment and scalability. "To keep growing, you have to keep raising the stakes and investing in your vision," he advises aspiring content creators. His journey reflects the power of resilience and the impact of continually striving for excellence.

## A New Paradigm in Online Philanthropy

Looking ahead, Donaldson remains committed to pushing the boundaries of digital content creation. He envisions further growth and innovation, including expanding his philanthropic efforts and exploring new business ventures. His focus includes leveraging his platform to drive positive change and inspire others to pursue their creative passions.

Donaldson's influence extends beyond YouTube. He actively supports initiatives that promote environmental conservation, education, and community support, reflecting his belief in the power of digital platforms to drive meaningful impact. His work has inspired a new generation of content creators to think big and use their influence for good.

## Conclusion

Jimmy Donaldson's story is a powerful example of how creativity, resilience, and a commitment to innovation can lead to extraordinary success. From his early challenges in launching MrBeast to building a transformative content empire, Donaldson's journey is marked by bold decisions and an unwavering dedication to his vision. His ability to navigate intense challenges and turn opportunities into transformative success has set a new standard in the digital content industry. Donaldson's journey serves as an inspiring reminder that with determination and a clear mission, any obstacle can be overcome.

# Tobi Lütke

## Coding His Way to E-Commerce Revolution

Born in 1980 in Koblenz, Germany, Tobias "Tobi" Lütke showed an early interest in technology. At just 12 years old, he was rewriting the code of video games he played, demonstrating a natural talent for coding and software development. This early interest paved the way for his future entrepreneurial journey.

## From Snowdevil to Shopify

In 2002, Lütke moved to Canada and met his future business partners, Daniel Weinand and Scott Lake. Initially, they planned to open an online snowboard equipment store called Snowdevil. However, frustrated by the existing e-commerce solutions that were too expensive or complex for small businesses, they decided to create their own platform. This decision led to the creation of Shopify in 2006.

## One Store at a Time

Lütke used his programming skills to develop a user-friendly interface that allowed users to customize their online stores without advanced technical knowledge. Quickly, the platform's flexibility and scalability attracted a wide range of users, from small startups to large companies.

One of the most notable decisions was to open Shopify to external developers, allowing them to create and sell apps that extended the platform's functionality. This initiative transformed Shopify into a versatile and modular platform, attracting a growing number of merchants and developers.

## Riding the Waves

Shopify's growth was not without obstacles. Lütke and his team faced fierce competition from e-commerce giants like Amazon and eBay. Additionally, they had to continuously innovate to meet the changing needs of their users and rapid technological advancements.

A particularly intense moment came during the 2008 financial crisis. Despite a challenging economic environment, Shopify continued to grow due to its commitment to innovation and customer satisfaction. Lütke's focus on a robust, user-centric platform helped Shopify stand out in a crowded market.

## Overcoming E-Commerce Challenges

In 2015, Shopify went public on the New York Stock Exchange, raising $131 million in its initial public offering. This milestone validated Lütke's vision and marked a significant step in his entrepreneurial journey. By 2021, Shopify had become the second-largest e-commerce platform in the United States, supporting over 1.7 million businesses worldwide. The COVID-19 pandemic in 2020 was another pivotal moment. While traditional brick-and-mortar businesses faced unprecedented challenges, Shopify experienced explosive demand as entrepreneurs and businesses turned to e-commerce. Shopify's ability to quickly adapt and support a massive influx of new merchants highlighted the platform's robustness and Lütke's foresight.

## Dodging Doughnuts

Shopify's mission is to make online entrepreneurship accessible to everyone. This mission is reflected in its policies and actions, such as the rule that employees caught checking the stock price must buy doughnuts for the team, aimed at maintaining focus on long-term vision rather than short-term fluctuations.

Shopify also emphasizes maintaining product integrity on its platform by enforcing acceptable use policies to ensure the quality and reliability of products sold. This commitment to quality has attracted traditional consumer goods companies like Unilever and Nestlé, drawn by Shopify's high-quality software and faster market access.

## Innovations and Social Commerce

Lütke and Shopify are at the forefront of e-commerce innovations. The platform anticipated trends such as online brands moving into physical stores, leading to the development of Shopify Point of Sale (POS) to support multi-channel selling. Additionally, Shopify Plus, aimed at larger businesses, operates separately to avoid diluting Shopify's entrepreneurial focus while enhancing global expansion and multi-location management.

Social commerce holds enormous potential, though current implementations are mainly ad-driven. Platforms like Facebook and Instagram play a key role, and Shopify differentiates itself by offering comprehensive e-commerce solutions beyond mere transaction processing, focusing on post-transaction logistics and customer service.

## The Heart of Entrepreneurship

Tobi Lütke's journey offers valuable insights into the power of innovation, "wrist-turner ideas", and customer focus. "Success is about solving real problems and having a significant impact," he often emphasizes. His ability to identify a market gap and build a platform that meets the needs of entrepreneurs highlights the importance of user-centered design and continuous improvement.

Lütke also stresses empowering entrepreneurs. "Our mission at Shopify is to make commerce better for everyone, so businesses can focus on what they do best: creating and selling their products," he advises aspiring entrepreneurs. His journey reflects the impact of creating a platform that prioritizes user experience and fosters business growth.

## Continuing to Innovate and Inspire

Looking ahead, Lütke remains committed to advancing Shopify's mission of empowering entrepreneurs worldwide. He envisions further growth and innovation, including expanding the platform's capabilities with new technologies like artificial intelligence and augmented reality.

Lütke's influence extends beyond Shopify. He actively supports initiatives promoting entrepreneurship and tech education, reflecting his belief in the power of business to drive positive change. His work has inspired a new generation of entrepreneurs to pursue their visions and create impactful solutions.

## Conclusion

Tobi Lütke's journey is a masterclass in innovation and perseverance. From a young coder in Germany to the visionary behind Shopify, his path is a vivid example of how passion and dedication can transform industries. Lütke's story is not just about building a successful company; it's about redefining e-commerce and democratizing entrepreneurship.

Despite facing significant challenges, from the financial crisis of 2008 to intense competition from industry giants, Lütke remained steadfast in his vision. His commitment to creating a user-friendly, scalable platform has empowered millions of entrepreneurs worldwide, turning Shopify into a cornerstone of modern e-commerce.

# Michelle Zatlyn

## From Canada to Silicon Valley: A Journey Begins

Born in 1981 in Saskatchewan, Canada, Michelle Zatlyn was raised in a supportive environment that emphasized education and hard work. Her academic journey took her from McGill University, where she earned a degree in Chemistry, to Harvard Business School, where she refined her entrepreneurial skills. This unique blend of scientific and business expertise set the stage for her future success in the tech industry.

## Eureka Moment: The Birth of Cloudflare

Zatlyn's entrepreneurial spark ignited at Harvard, where she met Matthew Prince and Lee Holloway. United by a common interest in cybersecurity, they recognized the growing threats of cyberattacks and inefficiencies in existing solutions. In 2009, they co-founded Cloudflare with the mission to build a better, safer internet. "We saw an opportunity to democratize security and performance for everyone online," Zatlyn recalls.

## Showdown at TechCrunch Disrupt

Cloudflare officially launched in 2010, offering a revolutionary service that combined security, performance, and reliability into a single platform. This innovative approach allowed businesses of all sizes to benefit from enterprise-level security without the associated complexity and cost. A pivotal moment came when Cloudflare impressed judges and the audience at the TechCrunch Disrupt startup competition, gaining significant momentum.

## Battling the Cyberstorm

Building Cloudflare was fraught with challenges, from skepticism and fierce competition to scaling operations while maintaining high standards. One particularly intense period came in 2012 when Cloudflare successfully defended against one of the largest DDoS attacks ever recorded, proving the robustness of their solution. Zatlyn's leadership and crisis management were crucial during these times. She noted, "Early on, facing disbelief or skepticism is common. Instead of taking it personally, focus on persisting and proving your worth."

## Scaling New Heights

Cloudflare's growth was rapid and remarkable. By 2020, the company had millions of customers and expanded its services significantly. Cloudflare became a cornerstone of internet infrastructure, protecting over 27 million internet properties and stopping over 70 billion cyberattacks daily. The company's IPO in 2019, valued at over $4 billion, marked a significant milestone, highlighting the collective effort of its team. "Don't fixate on winning over skeptics or seeking validation. Concentrate on making progress and finding supporters who champion your ideas," Zatlyn advises.

## Wisdom from the Frontlines

Michelle Zatlyn's journey offers valuable insights into the power of innovation, resilience, and strategic thinking. "Success is about creating solutions that solve real problems and make a meaningful impact," she emphasizes. Her focus on customer needs and continuous improvement highlights the importance of adaptability and perseverance.

## Eyes on the Prize

Looking forward, Zatlyn remains dedicated to advancing Cloudflare's mission of a safer internet. She envisions leveraging AI and machine learning to provide more intelligent security solutions and expanding Cloudflare's services to address emerging threats. Her commitment to innovation and growth continues to drive the company's success.

## Beyond the Firewall

Michelle's influence extends beyond Cloudflare. She actively supports initiatives that promote women in technology and entrepreneurship, reflecting her belief in the power of diversity and inclusion to drive positive change. Her work inspires the next generation of leaders to pursue their visions and create impactful solutions.

# Conclusion

Michelle Zatlyn's journey exemplifies the power of vision and perseverance. From a chemistry student in Saskatchewan to a cofounder of one of the most influential cybersecurity companies in the world, her path has been marked by innovation and relentless dedication. Cloudflare's rise from a startup to a critical component of global internet infrastructure underscores the impact of Zatlyn's leadership and foresight. Her ability to navigate challenges and spearhead advancements in cybersecurity has set a new benchmark in the industry.

Zatlyn's commitment to leveraging cutting-edge technologies and her advocacy for diversity and inclusion continue to inspire. Her story is a compelling reminder that with a clear vision and unwavering determination, it is possible to turn ambitious ideas into groundbreaking realities, thereby securing not just the internet but paving the way for future technological advancements.

# Ryan Trahan

## Crafting a YouTube Empire with Creativity and Grit

Ryan Trahan was born on October 7, 1998, in Eagle Lake, Texas, a small town where big dreams often seemed out of reach. Growing up, Ryan was deeply influenced by the tight-knit community and the values of hard work and perseverance instilled in him by his family. His early life was marked by a love for running and athletics, which later played a pivotal role in his journey to success.

## Ditching the Track for a YouTube Pack

Ryan's initial claim to fame wasn't YouTube but rather his prowess in athletics. A talented long-distance runner, he received a scholarship to Texas A&M University. However, a conflict with the NCAA's regulations over his YouTube earnings forced him to make a tough decision. Ryan chose to leave the university and pursue his passion for content creation full-time. This pivotal moment underscored his belief in following one's dreams despite the odds.

## Penny for Your Thoughts, or a YouTube Goldmine?

Ryan's YouTube journey began with fitness and lifestyle videos, leveraging his athletic background to build an audience. His early content focused on running tips, fitness challenges, and personal vlogs, gradually attracting a dedicated following. However, it was his creativity and willingness to take risks that truly set him apart.

One of Trahan's early breakthroughs came with his unique and engaging approach to content creation. He combined humor, creativity, and authenticity to produce videos that resonated with a wide audience. His willingness to take on outrageous challenges and document his journey with honesty and humor set him apart from other YouTubers.

One of the most dramatic moments in his YouTube career came with the viral "Penny Challenge" series. The impending extinction of the penny sparked the idea for the series, aiming to create excitement around a soon-to-be rare item. In this series, Ryan documented his journey across America with just a penny, trading and negotiating to survive. This series showcased not only his ingenuity and resilience but also his ability to connect with viewers on a personal level. The success of these videos propelled his channel into the mainstream, earning millions of views and a significant subscriber base.

## Tackling Turbulence

Building a successful YouTube channel was not without its challenges. Ryan faced numerous obstacles, including the pressure to constantly innovate and the scrutiny that comes with a growing public profile. One particularly intense period came when he faced backlash for some of his content decisions, which forced him to reflect and adapt his approach.

Ryan's ability to learn from criticism and remain authentic to his values has been crucial in maintaining his success. He emphasizes transparency with his audience, often sharing his struggles and growth process, which has endeared him further to his fans.

## Beyond the Screen

Ryan's success on YouTube has opened doors to various opportunities beyond the platform. He has launched his own merchandise line, collaborated with other influencers, and ventured into entrepreneurial endeavors. His focus on creating meaningful and engaging content has continued to drive his growth, making him one of the most influential creators of his generation.

One of the most significant milestones in his career came when he reached 10 million subscribers, a testament to his hard work, creativity, and the strong connection he has built with his audience.

## The Trahan Mantra: Passion Over Profit

Ryan Trahan's journey offers valuable insights into the power of resilience, innovation, and authenticity. "Success is about more than just numbers; it's about the impact you have on people's lives," he often emphasizes. His ability to combine entertaining content with genuine messages of perseverance and positivity highlights the importance of staying true to oneself. Ryan decided to emphasize the shift towards purpose-driven content creation, prioritizing passion over profit and focusing on meaningful storytelling. "Not always think about the better CTA, better thumbnail or anything," he explains.

Ryan also stresses the importance of adaptability and continuous learning. "You have to be willing to evolve and embrace change, both personally and professionally," he advises aspiring creators. His journey reflects the power of persistence and the impact of building a brand that resonates deeply with its audience.

## Future Ventures

Looking ahead, Ryan remains committed to expanding his creative horizons and using his platform to inspire others. He envisions further growth and innovation, including exploring new content formats and leveraging emerging technologies to enhance viewer engagement.

Ryan's influence extends beyond YouTube. He actively supports initiatives that promote mental health awareness and personal development, reflecting his belief in using his platform for good. His work has inspired a new generation of creators to pursue their passions and make a positive impact.

## Conclusion

Ryan Trahan's journey illustrates how passion, resilience, and authenticity can drive remarkable success. Overcoming early challenges with NCAA regulations to create a flourishing YouTube channel, his path is defined by bold decisions and steadfast dedication. Ryan's unique ability to engage his audience and transform obstacles into opportunities has redefined standards in the digital content landscape. His legacy stands as a testament to the power of determination and a clear vision, proving that with the right mindset, significant and meaningful change is possible.

# Julia Hartz & Kevin Hartz

## From Separate Paths to a Unified Vision

Julia, born on November 20, 1979, in Santa Cruz, California, was initially drawn to the arts and media. After graduating from Pepperdine University with a degree in telecommunications, she worked in television development, honing her skills at MTV and FX Networks. Kevin, born on October 5, 1970, in Berkeley, California, pursued a career in technology and finance. With degrees in history and applied earth sciences from Stanford University and a master's in finance from Oxford, Kevin co-founded Xoom Corporation, demonstrating his knack for entrepreneurship early on.

## The Spark

Julia's attraction to the tech industry grew during a long-distance relationship, prompting her to consider entrepreneurship. The concept for Eventbrite emerged from a simple yet powerful idea: democratizing event management and ticket sales. In 2006, Julia and Kevin, along with Renaud Visage, co-founded Eventbrite. The goal was to create an easy-to-use platform that would enable anyone to organize and sell tickets for events. Their vision was clear: empower event creators with tools previously accessible only to large organizations. Choosing to start Eventbrite meant risking financial stability for the chance to create their own destiny. Despite this risk, their commitment to the mission drove them forward. Eventbrite's mission to unite the world through live experiences became the inspiration and motivation for their team.

## A Journey of Innovation

Eventbrite's growth was fueled by innovation and a deep understanding of its users' needs. The platform's user-friendly interface and robust features quickly attracted a wide range of users, from small event organizers to large-scale festival planners. Julia's experience in media and entertainment helped shape the brand's voice and customer engagement strategies, while Kevin's background in finance and technology ensured the platform was scalable and reliable.

One key moment in Eventbrite's history was its response to the growing demand for mobile solutions. Anticipating the shift towards mobile, the team developed a comprehensive mobile app, allowing event organizers to manage their events on the go and attendees to purchase tickets seamlessly from their smartphones. Throughout its development, Eventbrite emphasized building an accessible, intuitive product while maintaining deep connections with customers and employees.

## Resilience in the Face of Adversity

Building Eventbrite wasn't without its challenges. The company faced intense competition from established ticketing giants like Ticketmaster. However, Julia and Kevin's commitment to their mission and their ability to pivot when necessary helped them navigate these obstacles.

One particularly challenging period was the COVID-19 pandemic, which brought the live events industry to a standstill. Eventbrite swiftly adapted by enhancing its virtual events capabilities, ensuring that creators could continue to connect with their audiences despite physical distancing measures.

Eventbrite's focus on the most important aspects and avoiding distractions has been integral to its DNA from the beginning. This focus helped them remain resilient and adaptable in the face of adversity.

## Eventbrite's Impact and Expansion

By 2018, Eventbrite had become a global leader in the event management space, facilitating millions of events across the world. The company went public in September 2018, raising $230 million in its IPO. This milestone validated the founders' vision and marked a significant achievement in their entrepreneurial journey.

## The Hartz Philosophy

Julia and Kevin Hartz's journey offers valuable insights into the power of vision, adaptability, and user-centric design. Julia often emphasizes the importance of perseverance and staying true to one's mission. "Success comes from creating something that people love and use every day," she says. Their ability to identify market gaps and build a platform that caters to those needs underscores the importance of innovation and customer focus.

Kevin, on the other hand, stresses the significance of resilience and strategic thinking. "Building a successful business requires navigating challenges and continuously evolving," he advises aspiring entrepreneurs. Their complementary skills and shared vision have been instrumental in Eventbrite's growth and success.

## Continuing to Innovate and Inspire

Looking ahead, Julia and Kevin remain committed to advancing Eventbrite's mission of empowering event creators worldwide. They envision further growth and innovation, including expanding the platform's capabilities with new technologies like artificial intelligence and enhancing its global reach.

Beyond Eventbrite, the Hartz couple actively supports initiatives that promote entrepreneurship, education, and innovation. Their work has inspired a new generation of entrepreneurs to pursue their visions and create impactful solutions.

## Conclusion

Julia and Kevin Hartz's journey is a shining example of how vision, resilience, and dedication to user needs can revolutionize an industry. From the initial challenges of launching Eventbrite to establishing it as a game-changer in event management, their story is characterized by bold choices and an unwavering commitment to their goals. Their adeptness at navigating adversity and transforming challenges into opportunities has redefined standards in the tech world. Julia and Kevin's legacy is a beacon of inspiration, demonstrating that with clear vision and relentless perseverance, obstacles can be surmounted, and significant innovation can be achieved. Their path serves as a motivating reminder that impactful success is within reach for those who dare to dream and act decisively.

# Emily Weiss

## Revolutionizing Beauty with Glossier

Born on March 22, 1985, in Wilton, Connecticut, Emily Weiss's story is a testament to the power of curiosity and creativity. Growing up, Emily was deeply influenced by her passion for beauty and fashion, which she nurtured through an early fascination with magazines and trends. Her early experiences in the industry, coupled with a deep understanding of consumer behavior, would later define her career. Weiss attended New York University, where she studied studio art, honing her creative skills and building a network in the fashion world. This innate curiosity set the stage for a career that would eventually revolutionize the beauty industry.

## From Intern to Beauty Mogul

Emily's journey began with a series of high-profile internships at renowned fashion magazines like Vogue and W Magazine. These experiences provided her with valuable insights into the industry and fueled her desire to create something impactful. While working as a fashion assistant at Vogue in 2010, she launched the blog *Into The Gloss*. The blog was a unique blend of beauty tips, interviews with industry insiders, and an honest look at beauty routines, quickly gaining a dedicated following. *Into The Gloss* became a go-to resource for beauty enthusiasts, establishing Weiss as a trusted figure in the beauty community.

## Crafting a Beauty Powerhouse

Inspired by the conversations and feedback from her blog's community, Emily saw an opportunity to create beauty products that resonated with real people. In 2014, she founded Glossier with the mission to make beauty more accessible and inclusive. Glossier's initial product line was directly influenced by the needs and preferences expressed by *Into The Gloss* readers. The brand launched with four core products: a face mist, a priming moisturizer, a skin tint, and a balm, celebrated for their minimalist design and user-friendly approach. The "Skin First, Makeup Second" philosophy resonated widely, setting Glossier apart in a crowded market.

## Innovating Through the Hurdles

Building Glossier was not without its challenges. Emily faced skepticism from traditional beauty brands and the pressures of creating a startup in a highly competitive industry. One of the most dramatic moments in Glossier's early history came when Weiss decided to launch the brand directly to consumers through e-commerce, bypassing traditional retail channels. This bold move allowed Glossier to build a direct relationship with its customers and gather valuable feedback to continually improve its products.

A notable moment of adversity was the launch of Glossier Play, a sub-brand aimed at colorful, playful makeup. Despite initial excitement, the line did not resonate as strongly with consumers, leading to its discontinuation. This experience underscored the importance of listening to customer feedback and being willing to pivot when necessary. Another intense period came during Glossier's rapid expansion, which required scaling production and maintaining the brand's core values. Emily's ability to innovate while staying true to her vision was crucial in navigating these challenges.

## Redefining the Beauty Landscape

Glossier's growth has been meteoric. By 2019, the company was valued at over $1 billion, making it one of the few female-led unicorns in the beauty industry. Emily's focus on community-driven product development and a direct-to-consumer model has been key to Glossier's success. The company had expanded its product line to include skincare, makeup, body care, and fragrance, becoming a beloved brand among beauty enthusiasts worldwide.

One of the most significant milestones in Glossier's journey was the opening of its flagship store in New York City. The store embodied the brand's ethos of inclusivity and engagement, providing a space for customers to experience Glossier products firsthand. This move reinforced the brand's commitment to creating a seamless online and offline experience. Another dramatic period came in 2019 when the company raised $100 million in a Series D funding round, valuing Glossier at over $1 billion. This milestone validated Weiss's vision and marked a significant achievement in her entrepreneurial journey.

## Emily Weiss's Beauty Playbook

Emily Weiss's journey offers valuable insights into the power of community, innovation, and resilience. "Success is about more than just creating products; it's about creating a connection with your customers," she often emphasizes. Her ability to engage with her audience and build a brand that reflects their needs highlights the importance of empathy and authenticity in business.

Emily also stresses the importance of adaptability and continuous improvement. "You have to be willing to listen, learn, and evolve," she advises aspiring entrepreneurs. Her journey reflects the impact of staying true to one's vision while being open to change. Her focus on community-driven innovation and authentic marketing played a key role in Glossier's success.

Weiss attributes Glossier's success to a combination of educating customers about product value and making strategic distribution decisions, which contributes to offering quality products at accessible prices.

## Beyond the Gloss

Looking ahead, Emily remains committed to advancing Glossier's mission of democratizing beauty and celebrating individuality. She envisions further growth and innovation, including expanding the company's product offerings and enhancing its digital platform to provide even more personalized and engaging experiences for customers. Emily's focus on inclusivity and community-driven development continues to guide Glossier's evolution.

Emily's influence extends beyond Glossier. She actively supports initiatives that promote female entrepreneurship and leadership, reflecting her belief in the power of business to drive positive change. Her work has inspired a new generation of entrepreneurs to pursue their passions and create meaningful connections with their customers.

## Conclusion

Emily Weiss's journey exemplifies how curiosity, resilience, and a commitment to community can drive remarkable success. From overcoming early challenges in the fashion world to establishing a groundbreaking beauty brand, her path has been defined by bold choices and steadfast dedication to her vision. Her skill in transforming obstacles into opportunities has set a new benchmark in the beauty industry. Weiss's legacy is a powerful reminder that with clear goals and unwavering determination, significant and meaningful achievements are within reach.

# Marc Benioff

## Early Life and the Seeds of Innovation

Marc Benioff was born on September 25, 1964, in San Francisco, California. Growing up in the heart of Silicon Valley, Benioff was immersed in technology from an early age. His passion for computers was evident as he programmed video games and sold them to pay for his tuition at the University of Southern California. This early exposure to technology and entrepreneurship set the stage for his future endeavors.

## Sparking a Revolution

Benioff's career began at Oracle, where he quickly rose through the ranks to become the company's youngest vice president. Despite his success at Oracle, Benioff felt a strong desire to create something new and transformative. Inspired by the burgeoning internet and the potential of cloud computing, he envisioned a new way for businesses to manage customer relationships.

In 1999, Benioff founded Salesforce with the mission to "end software" by providing customer relationship management (CRM) software through the cloud. This revolutionary approach allowed businesses to access their CRM tools online, without the need for expensive on-premises software installations. The idea was simple yet groundbreaking: make software accessible, affordable, and easy to use for companies of all sizes.

From this idea emerged a revolutionary concept that would take the world by storm, shifting the landscape from traditional installed-based software to SaaS products. Today, approximately 50,000 SaaS companies operate globally, providing cloud-based services on a monthly subscription model.

## Trailblazing in the Cloud

The early days of Salesforce were marked by innovation and a relentless focus on customer success. Benioff and his team developed the Salesforce platform with a user-friendly interface and powerful customization options, enabling businesses to tailor the software to their specific needs. They also introduced the concept of "No Software," emphasizing the simplicity and efficiency of cloud-based solutions.

One of the most dramatic moments in Salesforce's history came with the launch of its AppExchange in 2005. This online marketplace allowed third-party developers to create and distribute applications that integrated with Salesforce, significantly expanding the platform's functionality and creating a vibrant ecosystem. The AppExchange was a game-changer, solidifying Salesforce's position as a leader in the cloud computing industry.

## Against All Odds

Building Salesforce was not without its challenges. Benioff faced intense competition from established software giants like Microsoft and Oracle, as well as skepticism from potential customers who were wary of cloud-based solutions. Despite these obstacles, Benioff's vision and persistence paid off. He focused on creating a culture of innovation and customer-centricity, which helped Salesforce differentiate itself in a crowded market.

One particularly intense period came during the dot-com bust in the early 2000s. While many tech companies struggled or went out of business, Salesforce continued to grow by staying true to its core values and delivering exceptional value to its customers. Benioff's leadership and strategic thinking were crucial in navigating these turbulent times and positioning Salesforce for long-term success.

## Scaling New Heights

Salesforce's growth has been nothing short of meteoric. By 2020, the company had become the global leader in CRM software, with a market capitalization exceeding $200 billion. One of the most significant milestones in Salesforce's journey was its inclusion in the Dow Jones Industrial Average in 2020, a testament to its impact on the technology industry and the broader business world.

## Wisdom from the Trail

Marc Benioff's journey offers valuable insights into the power of innovation, resilience, and purpose-driven leadership. "Success is not just about making money; it's about making the world a better place," Benioff often emphasizes. His commitment to creating technology that empowers businesses while also driving positive social change highlights the importance of aligning business goals with broader societal objectives.

Benioff also stresses the importance of corporate social responsibility. Under his leadership, Salesforce has embraced the concept of the

"1-1-1 model," donating 1% of its equity, product, and employee time to charitable causes. This pioneering approach to philanthropy has inspired other companies to adopt similar models and has reinforced the idea that businesses can be powerful agents of change.

## Shaping the Future

Looking ahead, Benioff remains committed to advancing Salesforce's mission of driving digital transformation for businesses worldwide. He envisions further growth and innovation, including expanding Salesforce's capabilities through artificial intelligence and other emerging technologies. His focus on customer success and social impact continues to guide Salesforce's evolution.

Benioff's influence extends beyond Salesforce. He actively supports initiatives that promote equality, sustainability, and innovation, reflecting his belief in the power of business to drive positive change. His work has inspired a new generation of leaders to pursue their visions and create impactful solutions.

## A New Business Paradigm

Marc Benioff has also been a vocal advocate for stakeholder theory, which emphasizes the importance of focusing on stakeholders beyond just shareholders for business success. In an interview, he shared, "The reality is if I only focus on the shareholders, my company would be a disaster. The reason my company is successful is because I'm focused on my stakeholders, not my shareholders." He further elaborated, "The business of the business is improving the state of the world." These quotes highlight Benioff's belief in the broader role businesses should play in society.

# Conclusion

Marc Benioff's journey exemplifies how vision, resilience, and a dedication to making a positive impact can drive extraordinary success. His early challenges in establishing Salesforce transformed into a groundbreaking achievement, positioning the company as a global leader in cloud computing. Benioff's career is defined by his bold decisions and steadfast commitment to his mission, demonstrating an exceptional ability to navigate obstacles and leverage opportunities for lasting success. His legacy underscores the power of determination and a clear purpose, inspiring others to believe that any challenge can be overcome and that significant, meaningful change is within reach

# Evan Spiegel

## Pioneering Ephemeral Communication

Born on June 4, 1990, in Los Angeles, California, Evan Spiegel was raised in a family that valued education and creativity. His parents, both successful lawyers, instilled in him a strong work ethic and an appreciation for innovation. Spiegel attended the prestigious Crossroads School for Arts and Sciences in Santa Monica before enrolling at Stanford University, where his journey as a tech entrepreneur would begin.

## From Classroom Project to Tech Revolution

Spiegel's entrepreneurial journey began while he was studying product design at Stanford. In 2011, during a product design class, he teamed up with his fraternity brothers Bobby Murphy and Reggie Brown to work on a project that would eventually become Snapchat. The idea was born out of a simple yet revolutionary concept: a messaging app that would allow users to send photos and videos that would disappear after being viewed. This concept challenged the prevailing norms of social media, where content was typically permanent and meticulously curated.

The initial prototype, known as "Picaboo," was met with skepticism by peers and professors. However, Spiegel and his co-founders saw the potential for a platform that offered ephemeral messaging as a way to encourage more authentic and spontaneous communication. They rebranded the app as "Snapchat" and launched it in September 2011.

## Snapping Up Success

Snapchat's growth was rapid and transformative. Spiegel's vision of creating a platform that prioritized user experience and innovation was evident in the app's continuous evolution. Features like Stories, Discover, and Lenses (augmented reality filters) set Snapchat apart from other social media platforms and solidified its position as a leader in the tech industry. Spiegel has said, "Snapchat isn't about capturing the traditional Kodak moment. It's about communicating with the full range of human emotion — not just what appears to be pretty or perfect."

Snapchat's philosophy revolves around deeper relationships and self-expression, opposing traditional social media's focus on likes and attention. The company believes its values are difficult to copy because they are deeply ingrained and felt, especially through its strong community relationships. One of the most dramatic moments in Snapchat's history came with the launch of Stories in 2013, allowing users to share photos and videos that could be viewed for 24 hours. This feature was revolutionary, changing the way people shared their daily lives online and inspiring other platforms like Instagram to adopt similar features.

## Innovating Through Challenges and Competition

Building Snapchat was not without its challenges. Spiegel faced significant obstacles, including intense competition from tech giants like Facebook, which attempted to acquire Snapchat for $3 billion in 2013. Despite the lucrative offer, Spiegel declined, believing in Snapchat's potential for long-term growth. He famously said, "And after hearing hilarious stories about emergency detagging of Facebook photos before job interviews and photoshopping blemishes out of candid shots before they hit the Internet (because your world would crumble if anyone found out you had a pimple on the 38th day of 9th grade), there had to be a better solution."

One particularly intense period came when Instagram, owned by Facebook, introduced Stories, directly competing with Snapchat's core feature. Despite the competitive pressure, Spiegel's focus on innovation and user engagement helped Snapchat maintain its unique identity and loyal user base. Snapchat's response to imitation is continuous innovation and delivery of products that customers love, focusing on listening to and satisfying their needs.

## The Snapchat Phenomenon

Snapchat's success has been meteoric. By 2021, the app had over 500 million monthly active users and had become a major player in the social media landscape. Spiegel's emphasis on privacy, creativity, and user engagement has been crucial in maintaining Snapchat's relevance and appeal. "We're building a photo app that doesn't conform to unrealistic notions of beauty or perfection but rather creates a space to be funny, honest or whatever else you might feel like at the moment you take and share a Snap," Spiegel explains.

One of the most significant milestones in Snapchat's journey was its initial public offering (IPO) in March 2017, which valued the company at approximately $24 billion. This achievement validated Spiegel's vision and marked a significant milestone in his entrepreneurial journey.

## Evan Spiegel's Blueprint for Success

Evan Spiegel's journey offers valuable insights into the power of innovation, resilience, and user-centric design. "Success is not just about making money; it's about creating something that people love and use every day," Spiegel often emphasizes. His ability to identify and address a gap in the market highlights the importance of innovation and perseverance.

Spiegel also stresses the importance of privacy and authenticity in digital communication. "People should be able to share moments and express themselves without the fear of permanent digital records," he advises aspiring entrepreneurs. His journey reflects the power of staying true to one's vision while continuously evolving to meet user needs.

## The Future of Snap Inc.

Looking ahead, Spiegel remains committed to advancing Snap Inc.'s mission of empowering people to express themselves and live in the moment. He envisions further growth and innovation, including expanding the company's augmented reality capabilities and exploring new ways to enhance visual communication.

Spiegel's influence extends beyond Snapchat. He actively supports initiatives that promote technology education and entrepreneurship, reflecting his belief in the power of innovation to drive positive change. His work has inspired a new generation of entrepreneurs to pursue their visions and create impactful solutions in the tech industry.

## Conclusion

Evan Spiegel's journey showcases how vision, resilience, and a focus on user-centric design can drive extraordinary achievements. From navigating the early hurdles of launching Snapchat to establishing it as a pioneering force in social media, Spiegel's path is defined by bold choices and a steadfast commitment to his goals. His ability to face significant challenges and transform opportunities into sustained success has revolutionized the tech industry. Spiegel's story is a testament to the idea that with determination and a clear vision, any challenge can be surmounted, paving the way for groundbreaking innovation.

www.ingramcontent.com/pod-product-compliance
Lightning Source LLC
Chambersburg PA
CBHW071449220526
45472CB00003B/729